The Governors
and the New Federalism

The Governors
and the New Federalism

Marshall Kaplan
and Sue O'Brien

Westview Press

BOULDER • SAN FRANCISCO • OXFORD

This Westview softcover edition is printed on acid-free paper and bound in library-quality, coated covers that carry the highest rating of the National Association of State Textbook Administrators, in consultation with the Association of American Publishers and the Book Manufacturers' Institute.

Copyright © 1991 by Westview Press, Inc.

Published in 1991 in the United States of America by Westview Press, Inc., 5500 Central Avenue, Boulder, Colorado 80301, and in the United Kingdom by Westview Press, 36 Lonsdale Road, Summertown, Oxford OX2 7EW

A CIP catalog record for this book is available from the Library of Congress.

ISBN 0-8133-8371-4

Printed and bound in the United States of America

The paper used in this publication meets the requirements of the American National Standard for Permanence of Paper for Printed Library Materials Z39.48-1984.

10   9   8   7   6   5   4   3   2   1

Contents

v

Preface

During the height of the federal government's attack on American social problems in the 1960s and 1970s, scholars and practitioners frequently asked, "What about the states?" Doubts that the states could be counted on to make social policy seemed confirmed by reality. Governors and their aides were rarely asked to attend federal policy conferences in Washington. Very few states seemed to care about the tremendous growth in federal aid programs directed at poverty and social-welfare issues. Federal/city relationships supplanted federal/state linkages, constituting, in effect, a de facto constitutional amendment.

This situation was reversed in the 1980s, as the Reagan years brought about many significant and seemingly long-lasting changes in federalism, or the relationship between federal, state, and local governments. Clearly, states and local governments can no longer count on Washington for significant automatic budget increases for social-welfare initiatives. Just as clearly, they cannot look to the federal government for sustained leadership regarding new social-welfare policies and programs.

In many respects, the action shifted to the states in the 1980s. States have been pushed and, in some cases, have pushed themselves to the forefront of health, education, and welfare policy making. Their involvement was precipitated by the Reagan administration's budget cutbacks and efforts to cycle many federal aid programs through the states. State involvement was also precipitated by the economic and fiscal problems facing many local governments, particularly in the early part of the decade.

This book results from a Ford Foundation grant to the Graduate School of Public Affairs (GSPA) at the University of Colorado in Denver. It focuses on the leadership role played by eight governors in developing new or maintaining existing health, education, and welfare policies and programs. It purposely concentrates more on why and how governors acted than on the specifics of individual programs. It attempts to broadly classify different gubernatorial roles and their impacts on different kinds of policy development. Finally, to the extent possible, it relates the role of the governor to the political, economic, and institutional environment in each of the studied states.

We hope the book will provide governors, their staffs, and individuals interested in state government with insights into the relationship between varied modes of leadership and results. We also hope it will help present and future governors identify the decision-making processes that work best for them, their administration, and the citizens of their state. Finally, we hope the book will stimulate further research into the role of governors in setting policy and in developing programs.

The book is divided into three parts. Part One provides a brief overview and analysis of the relationship between Reagan administration initiatives and the states. It indicates that states had to contend simultaneously with new social-welfare responsibilities and with federal budget reductions and changing federal regulations governing health, education, and welfare assistance. Part Two presents mini case studies on the reaction of eight governors to federal health, education, and welfare policies and programs during the 1980s. It suggests links between different gubernatorial approaches to leadership and different state responses to national initiatives. Part Three compares the approaches of each of the studied governors and summarizes the findings on how economic, institutional, and political environments shaped the governors' responses to federal policy and program changes. It also provides brief observations on the effect of the governors' leadership on state bureaucracies and on state health, education, and welfare policies and programs.

We would like to thank the National Governors' Association and the Education Commission of the States for their help and support during this study. We are also grateful to Governors Lee Dreyfus, John Evans, William Janklow, Richard Lamm, Richard Snelling and William Winter for their willingness to participate in the oral-history colloquium that helped generate the data for this book. All these governors, plus Governors Michael Dukakis and Mark White, deserve our appreciation for agreeing to be the subjects of case studies. Dr. Robert Reischaur, Brookings; Dr. Ted Marmor, Yale; Dr. Frank Newman, Educational Commission of the States; and Dr. Ray Sheppach and Barry Van Lare of the National Governors' Association are to be thanked for interviewing the governors and joining the colloquium. We also want to acknowledge our colleagues at the University (Dr. Paul Bauman, Beth Lehr, Ken Torp, Carl Norbeck, State Senator Jack Fenlon) and NGA (Kelley Donley French) for their work on the case studies. Finally, but no less significantly, we want to extend our appreciation to Dr. Peggy Cuciti for describing the relationship between the states and the New Federalism, and to K.C. Mason for serving as our staff editor for the case studies.

Marshall Kaplan
Sue O'Brien

PART ONE

The States and the New Federalism

1

The Reagan Years and the States[1]

"The action is back in the local area and that's where the solutions have to be found," said former U.S. Senator Lawton Chiles, the latest in a long line of federal officeholders seeking to move to the state or local level.   In the words of David Broder, nationally syndicated columnist, the movement from Washington to the states "speak[s] volumes about where people of talent and integrity think they can make their best contribution these days. Hint: It's not in Washington."[2]

Some observers would go further, arguing that the real change is in the role of state governments. As noted by Richard Nathan, there has been "a fundamental shift in the balance of power and responsibility in American federalism . . . the enhancement of the role of state governments vis-à-vis both the national and local governments."[3]

The increasing importance of the states is attributed in large part to changes in federal policy initiated by President Ronald Reagan. He came into office committed to a new view of intergovernmental relationships. In his first inaugural, he spoke of his intention to "curb the size and influence of the federal establishment and to demand recognition of the distinction between the powers granted to the federal government [and] those reserved to the states or to the people." As part of President Reagan's New Federalism initiative, major changes in the structure of the grant system were proposed and enacted. Even more ambitious later efforts to reallocate responsibilities, however, failed.

President Reagan's New Federalism

To understand the shift in the balance of power in the federal system, one must look at fiscal policy and regulatory program changes as well as the programmatic shifts put forward as part of the president's New Federalism initiative.

1

Fiscal Policy

The pre-eminent concern of the Reagan administration was to reduce the role of government in the domestic sector. Governmental programs and the magnitude of taxes needed to support those programs were seen as important contributors to the economic problems that had beset the nation throughout the 1970s. To increase productivity, additional investment was required. To stimulate this investment and the savings required to support it, the administration recommended substantial cuts in marginal income tax rates.

With the passage of the Economic Recovery Tax Act of 1981 (ERTA), the president secured much of what he wanted (and perhaps more) in the way of tax code changes. Individual income tax rates were cut and bracket definitions were indexed for inflation. There were even deeper reductions in business taxes, especially in provisions affecting investment. The federal revenue loss was substantial, estimated as high as $1 trillion over a several year period.[4]

At the same time as taxes were reduced, the administration proposed large build-ups in the nation's defense capabilities. The combination of lower revenues and increased defense spending meant that very large reductions in domestic programs were required to bring the budget into balance.

The Omnibus Budget Reconciliation Act of 1981 (OBRA) made significant budget cuts—but these cuts were not evenly distributed across programs (see Table 1.1). As indicated above, there were increases in defense and in interest payments required to support the national debt. The large cuts were in direct federal operations and in grants to state and local governments for purposes other than low-income assistance. Means-tested entitlement programs providing benefits to low-income individuals were also cut back substantially. Social insurance programs, with their larger and politically stronger middle-income constituencies, took a somewhat smaller percentage of cuts.

A longer-term perspective on budgetary changes shows similar patterns (see Table 1.2). The deepest cuts were in programs providing support for state and local services and for the operations of federal domestic programs. Payments to individuals increased, especially in the social insurance programs.

While many budget cuts were proposed over the years, and a number were adopted (especially at the beginning of the Reagan administration), they were not enough to prevent the recurrence of very large deficits. The effect of OBRA and ERTA over the long term was to shift Washington's attention from problems and programs to the budget. The deficit problem effectively precluded the federal government from taking an active role in solving public problems, thereby forcing the initiative to other levels of government.

TABLE 1.1 Effect on Federal Budget Outlays in FY82 of Policy Changes Made in the First Year of the Reagan Administration by Major Budget Category

Budget Category	Baseline Outlays[a] (in billions of $)	Enacted Changes Relative to % of Baseline (in billions of $)	
National Defense	182.8	7.3	4.0
Benefit Payments for Individuals:			
Low Income Assistance	74.9	-5.5	-7.3
Social Insurance and Other	291.5	-9.6	-3.3
Other Grants to State and Local Governments	57.7	-8.4	-14.6
Net Interest	83.9	1.1	1.3
Other Federal Operations	72.5	-8.1	-11.2

[a] The baseline is an estimate prepared by the Congressional Budget Office of what outlays would be required to carry out the budget policies in place in the previous year.

Source: Data in the table compiled from John L. Palmer and Gregory B. Mills, "Budget Policy," in *The Reagan Experiment,* ed. John L. Palmer and Isabel V. Sawhill (Washington, DC: The Urban Institute Press, 1982), 80.

TABLE 1.2   Changes in Federal Budget Totals During the Reagan Years
(in billions of constant 1982 dollars)

Outlays and Revenues	Fiscal Year		% Change
	1980	1989	
Outlays			
National Defense	164.0	255.9	56.0
Direct Payments to Individuals	287.3	359.7	25.2
Payments to Individuals via Grants to State and Local Governments	37.4	50.6	35.3
All Other Grants to State and Local Governments	68.4	42.6	-37.7
Net Interest	62.0	133.5	115.3
Federal Operations	103.8	93.8	-9.6
Total Outlays	699.1	907.1	29.8
Total Revenues	611.7	786.5	28.5
Deficit	87.3	120.6	38.1

Source: Budget of the United States Government, Fiscal Year 1990, Historical
Tables (Washington, DC. US Government Printing Office).

Grant Consolidation and Budget Cuts

Prior to 1980, there had been a fairly steady expansion in intergovernmental grant programs. The grant system had become increasingly
complex, involving well over 500 discrete programs, with many bypass-
ing the states and involving direct relationships between federal agencies and local governments or nonprofit organizations. Often grants
were for narrowly defined purposes, and extensive regulation accompanied the flow of funds. Decisions regarding which programs were to be
funded and at what funding level were often made by federal agency
personnel.

In his proposal for block grants, President Reagan picked up on a direction for reform suggested by President Nixon a decade earlier in the first

first incarnation of New Federalism. Reagan called for the consolidation of more than 70 grant programs into 7 block grants.

Had the block-grant proposal not been combined with the broader budget and economic policy program in the Omnibus Budget Reconciliation Act of 1981 (OBRA), it is very likely that Congress—with its individual committees and their links to the interests involved—would have rejected most of the changes. Forced with an up-or-down vote on the entire package, however, Congress gave the president much of what he wanted, and consolidated 76 different grant programs were into 9 block grants. Key provisions of the block grants are summarized in Table 1.3.

Later efforts to consolidate additional grant programs generally failed to receive congressional support. Through 1986, President Reagan made 27 separate additional block-grant proposals; none passed, however, except the Job Training Partnership Act.

The block grants that were enacted had several important features.

- *The consolidation was accompanied by a significant cut in the level of funding.* While the president had proposed an average cut in spending of about 25 percent, Congress approved reductions averaging about 12 percent.[5] The magnitude of cuts varied by program.

- *The block grants tended to increase the role of the state government.* The state was usually the recipient of the block grant funds, although some consolidated grants went directly to local governments or other providers of service.

- *Block grants were distributed by formula.* This reduced the role of federal administrators in determining how and where the money was spent.

- *There was a significant reduction in federal regulations accompanying the flow of funds.* In education, 667 pages of regulations governing the 33 programs that were folded into the block grant were replaced by 20 pages. Each of the health block grants was covered by just 6 pages of regulations.[6]

- *A certain percentage of the funds distributed under several of the block grants could be redirected to other purposes at the option of the states.* This increased state discretion regarding the types of programs to be supported and how to apportion cuts.

TABLE 1.3 Summary of Block Grants Initiated in 1981 (in millions of dollars)

Block Grant	% Change		Number of Programs Consolidated[a]
	FY82 Appropriation	From FY81 Appropriation	
Alcohol, Drug Abuse and Mental Health	428.1	-20.8	10
Maternal and Child Health	347.5	-23.5	9
Primary Care	246.3	-23.9	2
Preventive Health and Health Services	81.6	-12.4	7
Community Services	336.5	-35.9	7
State Community Development[b]	900.0	-	1
Social Services	2400.0	-19.8	2
Elementary and Secondary Education	470.7	-10.5	37
Low Income Home Energy Assistance[b]	1869.0	6.6	1

[a] The reported number of programs consolidated differs with program definition. This listing is derived from Office of Management & Budget, Catalogue of Federal Grant Assistance.

[b] These programs are included even though they do not involve a consolidation of several programs because they do involve a shift in the structure of the program and a shift in responsibility from federal administration to state administration.

Source: George Peterson, "The State and Local Sector," in *The Reagan Experiment*, ed. John L. Palmer and Isabel V. Sawhill (Washington, DC: The Urban Institute Press, 1982), 172.

Regulatory Programs

One of the major themes of the Reagan administration was a reduction in regulatory burdens. Indeed, regulations associated with many federal grant programs, especially those combined into the block grants, were reduced and simplified. But regulations governing federal assistance programs are just the tip of the iceberg when it comes to "regulatory federalism." The record on other aspects of intergovernmental regulation is more complicated.

The Advisory Commission on Intergovernmental Relations has developed a typology of intergovernmental regulation, which is presented in Table 1.4. There has been a marked change since 1969 in the way the federal government has related to state and local governments. The commission attributes this to the increased use of more intrusive, and more compulsory regulatory programs. Whereas one might have expected a clear shift toward less regulations with the advent of New Federalism, this trend never materialized.

TABLE 1.4 A Typology of Intergovernmental Regulatory Programs

Type	Description	Major Policy Areas Employed
Direct Orders	Mandate state or local actions under the threat of criminal or civil penalties	Public employment, environmental protection
Crosscutting Requirements	Apply to all or many federal assistance programs	Non discrimination, environmental protection, public employment
Crossover Sanctions	Threaten the termination or reduction of aid provided under one or more grant programs unless the requirements of another program are satisfied	Highway safety and beautification; environmental protection; health planning, handicapped education
Partial Pre-emptions	Establish federal standards, but delegate administration to states if they adopt standards equivalent to the national ones	Environmental protection, natural resources, occupational safety and helath, meat and poultry inspection

Source: U.S. Advisory Commission on Intergovernmental Relations, *Regulatory Federalism: Policy, Process, Impact and Reform*, Report A-95 (Washington, DC: Advisory Commission, 1984), 8.

In assessing the administration's record on regulatory federalism, Richard Nathan concluded that the administration found it difficult to remove many regulations but did change the way regulations were enforced. "On the whole, delays or inaction in enforcement of existing regulations, particularly for crosscutting regulations, have resulted in a less intrusive federal presence in the states."[7] GAO's conclusion was slightly different:

> Notwithstanding some Reagan administration efforts to reduce overall levels of intergovernmental regulation, the Congress, federal agencies, the courts and the administration continued to use all . . . forms of regulation to expand and strengthen federal regulatory efforts.[8]

In the category of "partial pre-emptions," there were significant changes over the course of the 1980s. In these programs, the federal government establishes minimal standards or regulations governing private activity but delegates administration of the program to the states so long as they adopt standards at least as strong as the national minimum standards. "During Reagan's first term, the federal government's formal delegation of regulatory authority to states increased rapidly in several partial pre-emption programs, and federal oversight of state performance was relaxed."[9] While there is some debate as to whether these shifts were the direct result of Reagan administration policy or a natural stage in the life cycle of programs, there is little doubt that state authority increased in a number of program areas—including air quality, surface mining and occupational health and safety.

In addition, legislation affecting several of the regulatory programs that involve states in administration was passed. These amendments complicated the states' tasks and added to their financial and administrative burden. For example, the U.S. Department of Agriculture created new requirements that affected the entry of packaging materials to meat processing plants and changed procedures for inspection, tagging and retention of cattle. These requirements increased the burden on states since they were the ones—not the federal government—with inspection and enforcement responsibilities.[10]

A number of new "direct orders" were imposed on state and local governments without compensation during the 1980s. These requirements were imposed in environmental legislation and other legislation passed during the 1980s. For example, safe drinking water regulations were strengthened, forcing local governments to initiate additional, expensive treatment processes.

Direct orders and partial pre-emptions increase state and local responsibilities but limit discretion. Activity and financing responsibility occur at the state or local levels, not the federal level. In that sense, the trend was to greater decentralization. But at the same time, the ability of elected officials at the state and local level to determine what is to be done is limited by these federal regulatory actions. From this perspective, actions taken during the 1980s ran counter to the theme of decentralization implicit in New Federalism.

Federalism as Means or Ends

Restoring balance in the federal system and enhancing state authority were clearly articulated goals of the Reagan administration. Scholars will long argue about the strength of this commitment. Some suggest federalism objectives were simply a convenient method of achieving another more deeply held value—the reduction of government in public life. Reagan wanted to devolve authority, it is said, because he believed that if states were responsible, less would be done. He expected spending and regulation both to diminish if states were in charge.

On the spending side, there was little the administration could do if states chose to raise taxes and replace lost federal dollars. In the regulatory arena, however, critics note that the president was often willing to sacrifice the notion of state authority if state actions posed an inconvenience to business interests. Businesses prefer less regulation to more regulation, but perhaps as important, they prefer uniformity to diversity. Hence business interests wanted the federal government to restrict state regulatory activities or pre-empt state authority altogether. "Such concerns have not been ignored by the Reagan administration, which has sided again and again with business interests. In a recent study of proposed federal pre-emptions, the administration was found to have 'supported moves to take regulatory powers from the states in nine of the twelve cases studied."[11] In every area, except banking and civil rights, federal pre-emption of state regulatory authority was on the rise.[12]

The Federal Policy Context for State Action

Key Policy Changes Affecting Welfare and Social Services

As noted earlier, programs providing assistance to low-income populations bore a disproportionate share of the budget cuts enacted in the early years of the Reagan administration. Later efforts to further reduce these programs tended to be rejected by Congress.

OBRA made significant changes designed to constrain the growth of programs such as Food Stamps, AFDC and Medicaid. The administration did little to reduce the benefits of what they defined as the "truly needy"—those with no income and those who were presumed unable to work. But it reduced benefits and restricted access to programs for those with some income. Hence the biggest impact was on the working poor.

Expenditure levels in means-tested entitlement programs are the result of key parameters set in law. Typically, access to a specific service or benefit level is guaranteed to all those who meet certain eligibility requirements. Both the federal government and the states play a role in setting eligibility and benefit parameters. Budgetary savings in the means-tested entitlement programs were sought in two ways: by changing rules specified in federal legislation and by encouraging states to change their laws.

AFDC: The Aid to Families with Dependent Children program provides cash payments to families with children if the families don't have sufficient income to cover basic needs. In some states, the program is restricted to single-parent families, while in others, two-parent families are eligible as well. The federal government pays a varying percentage of total program costs depending on the state and its income level.

OBRA included several changes in law affecting who would be eligible for AFDC benefits. First it put an income cap on eligibility for benefits. Households with gross earnings above 150 percent of the state-defined "need standard" would no longer be eligible for benefits. Second, provisions governing deductions from earned income that were important determinants of the size of an individual's welfare payment were changed. Specifically, the "thirty and a third" rule was eliminated after four months of eligibility.[13] Also the procedure for calculating work expenses was revised. These changes, along with the cap, are said to have reduced caseloads and expenditures by approximately 10 percent of what they would have been absent the changes.[14]

In effect the changes eliminated the provisions designed to encourage AFDC recipients to seek jobs. The administration preferred to substitute a "stick" for the "carrot," and it proposed requiring states to establish workfare programs. AFDC recipients would have been required to work off their benefits. While Congress rejected mandatory workfare, it did encourage states to experiment with various types of work requirements.

By 1985, some of the restrictions on AFDC eligibility were eased. Furthermore, a consensus emerged that the welfare system had to be reformed using a twofold strategy. The first part of the strategy adopted the conservative theme that welfare recipients should be required to make an effort toward self-sufficiency. The second part of the reform appealed to liberals; it required welfare agencies to provide education and training opportunities that would help welfare recipients obtain jobs with decent wages. The Family Support Act of 1988 was signed by President Reagan shortly before he left office.

Food Stamps: The food stamp program is essentially a federal program. The federal government sets rules regarding eligibility and benefits. It also pays the lion's share of total costs. States, however, are involved in administering the program and, as a result, may feel the heat for changes in program rules. Food stamps are sometimes thought of as the core of a national income-support system, with states supplementing the basic amount provided by the federal government via AFDC benefits or general assistance.

The policy changes enacted in 1981 reduced the number of people eligible for food stamps by placing a cap on gross income allowed for eligibility. It also reduced the deductions that could be made against gross income, thereby reducing the benefit level for many recipients, especially the working poor.

Block Grants: Other changes of importance were the cut in funding for the social services block grant and the reduction in regulations governing use of those funds. With the shift to the community services block grant, the states were given a role in dealing with the community action agencies, which had previously dealt directly with the federal government.

Key Policy Changes Affecting Health

Health policy has been a major concern at both the state and federal level for a number of years. There has been tremendous pressure on government to act to increase both access to and affordability of health care. Some initiatives in the health care area were discretely federal (Medicare), but others involved partnerships with state governments. For both levels of government, the cost of health programs has been increasing at a rapid rate, claiming larger shares of total budgets. For example, in the period immediately preceding the Reagan policy change—1965-1980—health spending almost tripled its share of the federal budget, rising from 4.5 percent to 11.8 percent. Health programs' share of state and local spending grew by about a third, from 6.9 percent to 9.3 percent.[15] Despite these increases, access to health services remained a problem for numerous people lacking private health insurance, as it still does today.

The Reagan administration initiated many changes in health policy to which states had to respond. Most important were changes in the Medicaid program, but also several of the smaller categorical grant programs were also restructured.

Medicaid: The Medicaid program provides a form of health insurance to certain poor people. Since eligibility for Medicaid is in part determined by eligibility for AFDC, the changes described above had spillover effects on the Medicaid program. Poor families declared ineligible for welfare also lost the health insurance previously provided through Medicaid. The cost savings were shared by the federal and state governments. The administration, however, sought additional savings in this program.

Medicaid has traditionally been structured as an open-ended grant program. The federal government pays a certain percentage of whatever a state spends to provide health services to eligible persons. The federal share varies, depending on a state's income level relative to the national average. Within certain constraints defined in federal law, the states determine which health services to provide and who is eligible to receive them.

The administration sought to cap this entitlement program by limiting the payment it would make to each state to a specified percentage of the prior year's spending. Congress rejected this approach but it did propose a reduction in the federal matching rate if expenditures in any given state rose by more than a specified percentage. States' authority to shape the Medicaid program and, hence, to control costs was also increased. For example, "They were given authority to design systems for reimbursing hospitals and other health care providers; to limit recipients' freedom to choose which provider they would use; and to define who would be served and what services they would be provided under the 'medically needy' portion of the program."[16]

Starting with the Deficit Reduction Assistance Act of 1984, Congress started undoing some of the restrictive measures imposed in 1981.[17] The subsidy reductions were ended and states were encouraged to expand Medicaid eligibility for certain needy non-AFDC women and children. This posed a challenge of a different kind to states.

Block Grants: Four of the block grants created in 1981 involved health programs. All involved substantial cuts in funding and a restructuring of traditional relationships among local governments, nonprofit providers, the states, and the federal government.

The Alcohol, Drug Abuse and Mental Health block grant consolidated three grant programs that had supported community mental health centers with several alcoholism and drug abuse treatment and prevention programs. The 1982 budget for these programs was 20.8 percent less than had been appropriated in 1981. The magnitude of the cuts varied by state, however; in one study of 14 states, cuts ranged from 0 to more than 25 percent.[18]

The Maternal and Child Health block grant combined nine categorical programs supporting crippled children, genetic testing, counseling and family planning, and lead paint poisoning prevention. The 1982 budget for these programs was 23.5 percent below 1981 levels. Again cuts varied considerably by state.

The Preventive Health and Health Services block grant combined seven existing programs covering such things as rodent control, hypertension control, emergency medical services, and health education. It also added a new component for rape prevention. Funding was 12.4 percent less than 1981 levels.

The Primary Care block grant funded community health centers. Involvement was a state option and few states chose to get involved.

Key Policy Changes Affecting Education

Education is somewhat different from the other areas we have discussed. In health and welfare, the federal government pays a significant share of total program costs. The federal funding role for elementary and secondary education, on the other hand, has traditionally been quite small relative to state and local roles. In 1980, federal spending was just 9.8 percent of the total governmental expenditure for elementary and secondary education.

In education, three developments in Washington set the context for state decision making. Two are similar to what we have discussed above: budget cutbacks and grant consolidation. The third development is quite different. State policy agendas were in part driven by a widely publicized national study that documented educational failure and recommended structural reform.[19]

Block Grants: President Reagan had called for the formation of two block grants. One would have combined several of the large educational grants that focused on special needs (e.g., Title I compensatory education and handicapped programs), while the other would have focused on resources and school performance. Congress rejected the first consolidation but accepted the second, which involved some 37 small categorical programs. States received the funds but were mandated to pass through 80 percent to local districts. As a result of the block grant, states could shift priorities and change the distribution among districts.

While Congress rejected some of the restructuring proposed by the president, it did enact significant budget cuts. The 1982 budget for educational programs was 26 percent less than the amount necessary to maintain 1981 service levels.

Simplification of regulation and reporting requirements was associated with many of the grants. On the other hand, some key requirements—such as the call for an appropriate education for all handicapped children—remained intact.

Efforts to Frame the Educational Reform Agenda: The Reagan administration also sought policies designed to encourage parent choice in education. It proposed a tuition tax credit for this purpose, but the idea was rejected by Congress. Nevertheless, the administration, through its use of the bully pulpit, kept various kinds of choice options on the policy agenda.

The administration also sought to reshape the educational reform movement, shifting its focus from issues of equity to performance. The National Commission on Excellence in Education, appointed by the president in 1981, published *A Nation At Risk* in 1983. Claiming the nation's economic future was at stake, the commission urged schools to toughen their standards, redirect their curricula back to basic academic subjects, and increase the time students spend on their studies. States were urged to take steps to improve the preparation of teachers and to make teaching a more rewarding profession. *A Nation At Risk* ensured a place on state policy agendas for issues such as teacher certification and pay, curriculum, and testing.

The States' Response

For the states, New Federalism posed both a challenge and a dilemma. Washington was offering greater responsibility but fewer resources. States responded in different ways depending upon their economies, political traditions, governmental structure, and leadership.

Institutionally and politically, the states' capacity to respond was much greater in 1980 than it had been in earlier years. Beginning in the 1960s, states had modernized their governmental structures, including reforms in all branches of government. They had reduced the number of elected officials and strengthened the policy role of the governor. The skills and training of state administrative personnel had increased. Likewise, numerous reforms had been made affecting legislatures and courts.[20]

From a fiscal perspective, the picture regarding states' capacity is mixed. Looked at over a longer time horizon, there had been a substantial strengthening of state capacity due to a diversification of revenue sources. Both sales and income taxes are highly responsive to economic growth and over the years states had increased their reliance on these two sources of revenue.

A shorter time perspective, however, suggests that many of the states were in a weak fiscal position in 1981 and 1982, when the Reagan policy changes were first initiated. The same tax revolt that had swept Reagan to power had taken its toll on the state and local sector. State and local own-source revenues as a percentage of personal income peaked in 1977.[21] The trend was clearly in the direction of reducing state and local tax rates. The states' response to New Federalism was further hampered by the economic recession of 1981-1982.

Faced with declining grant and own-source revenues, many states reversed their tax policy in 1982 and started raising rates or broadening the base of revenue collections. These actions put the states in a much stronger position once the economy turned around in 1983 and 1984.

There is no simple way to describe the response of the states to New Federalism. It varied by state and by program. According to Richard Nathan, three factors were most important in influencing the response:

> (1) the incidence of the benefits or services provided (2) the strength of a grant's constituency and the level of its general public support and visibility and (3) the "identification" in the minds of state and/or local officials of the grant program as "federal" or state and local.[22]

For the most part, it appears that little attempt was made at the state level to reverse the cuts in AFDC eligibility mandated by federal rule changes. This program was perceived as "federal" and in most states no strong constituency represented the working poor, who were most hurt by the cutbacks. Where Medicaid was concerned, states responded to the federal call to hold the line on expenditures by implementing aggressive cost-cutting strategies, while generally trying to maintain the level of services provided.

Many, but not all, of the services funded by the federal programs consolidated into the block grants were maintained despite the 1981 cutbacks. Several factors have been cited. First, there often were significant amounts of funding "in the pipeline"—authorized by the federal government in prior years but not yet spent by the states. With the shift in grant structure, prior-year funds could be melded with current-year grants. This and other forms of fancy footwork allowed the states to put off the day of reckoning. By 1983, there were some restorations of federal funding and some willingness on the part of the states to use their own revenues to replace lost federal grant funds. Social service programs and maternal and child health programs were most likely to be protected, while federal cuts were more likely to be "passed on" in the preventive health and community action programs.

Conclusion

The challenge faced by states in the 1980s was formidable. In his first years in office, President Reagan sought and obtained major changes in tax and budget policy. Programs providing financial assistance to state and local governments were substantially restructured to reduce the level of federal direction, but they were also cut back in size. Programs providing assistance to low-income families, particularly the working poor, were also cut back. States had to make decisions regarding which services to maintain and which to cut back, and whether to increase their own contributions to replace the loss of federal funding.

In the regulatory arena, the picture is complex. The level of regulation accompanying federal assistance programs clearly decreased. What we think of as federal regulatory policy, however, remained intact or grew more complicated. The burden on states as the implementors of many of these regulatory policies increased. Even though federal oversight may have decreased in some programs, state discretion remained quite limited.

Notes

1. This chapter was prepared by Dr. Peggy Cuciti.

2. As cited in "The Action Is All Local," editorial in *City and State*, 18 June 1990.

3. Richard P. Nathan, Fred C. Doolittle and Associates, *Reagan and the States* (Princeton, NJ: Princeton University Press, 1987).

4. John L. Palmer and Isabel V. Sawhill, "Perspectives on the Reagan Experiment," in *The Reagan Experiment*, ed. John L. Palmer and Isabel V. Sawhill (Washington, DC: The Urban Institute Press, 1982), 8.

5. Nathan, *Reagan and the States*, 58.

6. Timothy Conlan, *New Federalism: Intergovernmental Reform from Nixon to Reagan* (Washington, DC: Brookings Institution, 1988), 207.

7. Richard P. Nathan, Fred C. Doolittle, and Associates, *The Consequences of Cuts* (Princeton, NJ: Princeton University Press, 1983) 187.

8. U.S. General Accounting Office, *Federal-State-Local Relations: Trends of the Past Decade and Emerging Issues* (GAO/HRD-90-34) (Washington, DC: U.S. Government Printing Office), 4.

9. Timothy Conlan, *New Federalism: Intergovernmental Reform from Nixon to Reagan* (Washington, DC: Brookings Institution, 1988), 206.

10. See U.S. General Accounting Office, *Federal-State-Local Relations*, 29, for a recounting of several changes in law increasing the regulatory burden on state and local governments.

11. Felicity Barringer, "U.S. Pre-emption: Muscling in on the States,"

Washington Post, 25 October 1982. Cited in Conlan, *New Federalism*, 13.

12. U.S. General Accounting Office, *Federal-State-Local Relations*.

13. As an incentive to work, the AFDC law had allowed a family to keep $30 per month of its earnings plus one-third of the earnings above that amount. Absent this provision, a welfare family can lose one dollar in benefits for every dollar earned and thus receive no monetary benefit for its work effort.

14. Nathan, *Reagan and the States*, 57.

15. Judith Feder, John Holahan, Randall R. Bovbjerg, and Jack Hadley, "Health," in *The Reagan Experiment*, ed. Palmer and Sawhill, 187.

16. Nathan, *Reagan and the States*, 56.

17. George Peterson, "The State and Local Sector," in *The Reagan Experiment*, ed. John L. Palmer and Isabel V. Sawhill, 173.

18. Seven of the fourteen states were assigned to the category "lost 25-49% of funding." Nathan, *The Consequences of Cuts*, 38.

19. National Commission on Excellence in Education *A Nation At Risk: The Imperative for Educational Reform*, 1983. (Washington, DC: The Commission, U.S. Government Printing Office distributor), 24.

20. U.S. Advisory Commission on Intergovernmental Relations, *The Question of State Government Capability*, Report A-98 (Washington, DC: U.S. Government Printing Office, 1985).

21. Palmer, *The Reagan Experiment*, 162.

22. Nathan, *Reagan and the States*, 96.

PART TWO

The Case Studies:
Leadership, the New Federalism
and the Governors[1]

The New Federalism brought forth diverse responses from each of the fifty states. Some of the Governors used the Reagan initiatives as a catalyst to reform one or more public and private sector institutions delivering health, education and welfare services. Some of the Governors, out of ideological conviction or fiscal necessity, emphasized cut back management. Some of the Governors focused on standing at the gate; that is, they saw their role as protecting their state's basic social welfare commitments from Reagan era changes.

Many variables shaped each Governor's reaction to the administration's health, education and welfare policies and programs. Among them: the economic health of the state, the political history and traditions of the state, the powers—formal and informal—of the Governor's office, the personality and background of the Governor. In this context, no easy way exists to pick a representative sample of Governor's and or Governors' responses to the New Federalism.

The eight Governors chosen for case study in this chapter illustrate many different kinds of leadership approaches to the Reagan initiatives. Hopefully, they reflect the range of responses found in most, if not all, the 50 states to the key health, education and welfare proposals and actions of the Reagan administration. Clearly, they portray the effect the political, social, and economic environment of each state has on the Governor's leadership. Just as clearly, they suggest the difference personality, structure or form of governments and geography have on the Governor's perception of state problems and on his ability to respond to state problems. Finally, they provide a better understanding of the relationship between leadership style and leadership impact.[2]

Notes

1. The case studies in Part Two were drawn from more extensive material prepared by the following individuals: in Mississippi, Dr. Paul Bauman, Beth Lehr, GSPA; in Texas, Dean Marshall Kaplan, GSPA; in South Dakota, Carl Norbeck, GSPA; in Colorado, Ken Torp, GSPA; in Vermont, Ken Torp, GSPA; in Idaho, Dr. Paul Bauman, GSPA; in Wisconsin, Kelley Donley French, NGA; in Massachusetts, State Sen. Jack Fenlon, GSPA.

2. Staff initially arrayed all states according to the range of their responses to the health, education and welfare policies and programs of the Reagan Administration. The inventory of practitioners familiar with and interested in state government. Suggestions were recorded as to which states would be good to study. The eight case studies in this chapter resulted from this process. All of the Governor's initially identified for study agreed to be subject of the study. The case studies resulted from field visits to the studied state by staff and faculty, a review of background data relevant to the state and, importantly, from the oral history provided by many of the Governor's, themselves, at the colloquium referred to in the preface.

2

Mississippi

WILLIAM WINTER, DEMOCRAT, 1980-1984

Context

Mississippi entered the decade of the 1980s ranked last among the states by nearly every standard. Of its 2.6 million people, nearly one in four lived below the poverty level. Its per capita income was the lowest in the United States. It had one of the highest unemployment rates, the highest death rate, highest infant mortality, highest percentage of people receiving public aid, lowest welfare payments, lowest teacher salaries, highest dropout rate, and lowest per-pupil expenditure in grades K-12. Transfer payments from the federal government were the main source of income for almost half of Mississippi's 84 counties.

Blacks make up 35 percent of Mississippi's population, the highest percentage of any state. Mississippi's turbulent history is inexorably linked with black history—from earliest slavery, through the Civil War and Reconstruction, to the Voting Rights Act of 1965 and on to William Winter's historic education package of 1982.

Change occurs slowly in Mississippi. It was a decade behind other states in getting electricity to rural areas and mechanizing farming. Integrated schools were forced on the state by the federal government. Civil rights activists were murdered during the "Freedom Summer" of 1964.

Politically, Mississippi displays the southern, conservative banner of the Democratic Party.

Mississippi turned the corner on outmigration of its population in the late 1960s after desegregation took hold. The economy grew and the state lost its basic agricultural flavor. By 1980, more than half the state's work force held white-collar jobs.[1]

Constitutionally, Mississippi has a weak-governor system. The governor can veto legislative acts, but does not direct the budgetary process. Many state officials are elected rather than appointed by the governor.

The governor has little influence on many state agency directors, who are appointed by staggered-term boards named by previous governors. And until 1986, governors—including Winter—were limited to one term. The influence of a Mississippi governor comes from four sources: personal rapport with the legislature; the line-item veto; the ability to marshal public support; and control of most federal funds coming into the state.[2]

State government was mired in corruption and chaos when Winter was elected in 1979. Three state senators had served jail terms for influence peddling in federal human services programs. The administration of Winter's predecessor, fellow Democrat Cliff Finch, had become increasingly erratic. When he took over, Winter said, he found the office with "filing cabinets literally turned over and files destroyed."

A lagging economy worked against Winter from the beginning of his term. Because of overly optimistic revenue projections, Winter had to cut $70 million from the 1981 budget, $100 million from the 1982 budget, and another $80 million from the budget of 1983. Legislators had a strong aversion to raising taxes, which made his educational reform success story all the more remarkable.

Profile

Born 21 February 1923 in Grenada County, Winter was the only pupil in the history of his rural, segregated school to finish high school. He graduated from the University of Mississippi in 1943 and was elected to the Mississippi House of Representatives a year before he earned his law degree in 1949. He served in the U.S. Army during World War II.

Colleagues describe Winter as quiet, thoughtful, and precise in speech, retaining many of the traits of a "southern gentleman." He addresses people as "ma'am" and "sir," holds the door open for his guests and stands when women enter the room.

Early in his political career, Winter established himself as a supporter of equal rights for blacks. His reputation may have cost him being elected as governor in 1967 and 1975. By his third campaign in 1979, however, better education, new jobs, industry, and crime had replaced racial policy as priority issues and Winter was elected.

Winter firmly believed Mississippi never would improve economically until it increased its citizens' basic skills through education and training. In his view, the old solutions would not work, and fear of change no longer was tolerable.

Governing called Winter a delegator who left the day-to-day affairs of state government to his aides.[3] Assistant Dick Molpus said Winter "found trusted people who shared his vision and left them to their own devices." Molpus, who was later to be elected secretary of state, said many members of the "intensely loyal" staff had started as teenagers supporting Winter's political career. The group came to be known as the "boys of spring" because of their youth (the oldest was 31), their willingness to take risks and, as even Winter admitted, their occasional naiveté.

Education

Winter, generally a consensus seeker, was prepared to be confrontational about education.[4] He was aggressively involved in the fight for the $110 million education reform package that became the centerpiece of his term.

Early in the term, Winter became convinced that many of the state's problems—unemployment, high welfare caseloads, premature deaths—had the common denominator of low literacy. Winter determined that Mississippi needed to reduce the dropout rate and enforce a mandatory attendance law that had been virtually ignored. In just one year, Winter said, 3,000 potential first graders failed to show up for school.

Whereas previous governors had kept out of the way of the elected state superintendent of education and let the system run under its own momentum, Winter took an official leadership role in changing it. He appointed a 21-member panel of business, education, and legislative leaders to look at the status of education and give him suggestions for improvement.

The committee's December 1980 recommendations were all incorporated into the education reform package Winter presented in his 1981 State of the State address. Despite a recession and declining revenues, Winter sought a $100-million tax increase to pay for a complete overhaul of the school system. The package included free kindergarten for anyone who wanted it, increased teacher salaries, enforcement of compulsory attendance, and performance-based accreditation to raise curriculum requirements.

Selling educational reform to the legislature was difficult. Bitterness lingered over forced integration. Some lawmakers, believing blacks to be the primary beneficiaries of the proposal, clung to the plantation owner mentality that if you educate a field hand you ruin a good field hand.

No action was taken in 1981.

"The last thing the legislature wanted to do was raise taxes," said Winter. He also noted there was no time to build consensus before the 1981 legislative session.

Winter and the "boys of spring" mounted a public campaign for education reform and took the same package back to the 1982 legislature.

Still, the only item that passed was a constitutional amendment restructuring the state board of education and providing for future state superintendents to be appointed by a board controlled by the governor, lieutenant governor, and house speaker. Previously, the superintendent had been elected. It may have been more luck than Winter's influence that won the amendment's passage. The superintendent at the time was involved in a book-selling scandal and had little credibility.

It had appeared, however, that the entire package would pass until the speaker of the house took a voice vote on a motion for adjournment. Observers said the motion was overwhelmingly defeated, but the speaker gaveled the session to a close without permitting a vote on the reform package.

Winter used the statewide indignation over the speaker's action to build public support for his plan. Believing that if he lost the education package, he would be perceived as a weak and ineffectual governor, Winter drew up plans for what he called "the largest mass movement in the history of Mississippi." In the fall of 1982, 10 public forums were held around the state, attracting crowds of as many as 4,000 people. Winter then decided to "shoot the works" and seek passage of an identical package during a special session called for early December.

"If we were going to go down, we were going to go down with the guns a'blazin' and the engine on fire," said Molpus.

Powerful legislative leaders balked at the special session, both because they were against reform and because they did not want to consider raising taxes with an election year right around the corner. The Senate Finance Committee chairman said he would refuse to hold a committee meeting during the special session.

"There was a lot of subtle opposition based on racism," Winter said. "Kindergartens were perceived by many people as being a black babysitting enterprise. Some of the greatest resistance came from those counties where there had been white flight from public schools. Segregated academies were dominant and public schools really were attended mostly by black students."

Winter said some religious fundamentalists were against the plan because they believed kindergartens would "snatch the children from their mothers' arms." Landowners feared an increase in property taxes, even though property taxes were not directly involved. Energy-related businesses objected, even after a proposed increase in the oil and gas severance tax was dumped.

Grassroots support was mobilized. More than 25,000 citizens signed lists backing education reform. Winter's staff organized phone banks; the media rallied behind the effort; and private-sector funds were raised for television and radio advertising. PTA leaders talked about the package in schools; preachers had it in their sermons.

On 20 December 1982, Mississippi got its so-called "Christmas miracle." With the legislative leadership feeling constituent pressure, Winter's entire $110 million shopping list was passed during the special session. Most of the package was to be funded through increased sales and income taxes. It mandated a 10 percent increase in teachers' salaries, statewide free kindergarten, and school attendance until age 14.

Winter believes he caught legislators in a mood to make history because he ordered a three-year State Capitol renovation project completed one month earlier than had been scheduled, so it would be ready in time for the special session. "It came after three years of meeting in an abandoned high school, which was a totally uninspiring arena in which to do impressive things," he said.

Winter's success gave him a different relationship with the legislature, and the last year of his term was his most productive. Winter regrets being unable to carry the momentum into a second term. But in an ironic note, Winter said he probably would not have called for the special session had he been able to run for reelection and use education reform as a campaign issue.

Health

The effort to meet the challenge of New Federalism, particularly in health and welfare, fit Winter's own definition of reform: "finding within the framework of existing programs a basis of change that would enable those programs to operate in a more effective way, creating a more satisfactory and more equitable delivery of services and creating a result that would be of benefit to a greater number of people."

Winter inherited a state health department that ran smoothly, but was hard pressed to deliver adequate services because of limited funding. However, because of the mismanagement of state government during the previous administration, Winter's first need was to rebuild trust. Through a series of public meetings across the state, Winter and his cabinet sought to explain the distribution of federal block grants and how things could change under Ronald Reagan.

"The compelling need in the field of health was to try to reduce the number of agencies involved in the various health delivery enterprises," Winter said. Shortly after his inauguration, Winter consolidated several smaller health and welfare agencies, firing 23 directors and deputy directors in the process. The action got legislative approval with little opposition.

Winter delegated the job of reorganizing the Department of Health to its director, Dr. Alton B. Cobb, a very able administrator who both developed ideas and initiated health care policy. "I took my lead from him," said Winter. The department, with Winter's support, administratively created a new fee system to raise more revenue. A surcharge was imposed on some health services, contingent upon a client's ability to pay. Another $1 million was raised for an Emergency Medical Service operating fund by imposing a $5 surcharge on all moving traffic violations.

With additional revenue from the special fees, counties were able to match community block grants that Winter made available under New Federalism guidelines. Much of the grant money was used to renovate or build county-owned health care facilities. In all, 40 new health care facilities were built during Winter's term.

Another Winter priority was to use federal transfer payments on nutrition programs to reduce the infant mortality rate, the highest in the country. Winter funnelled as much money as possible to the health department for the Women and Infant Children (WIC) program.

Medicaid was another source of federal revenue for the state, but Winter had little to do with administering the program. During his term, Medicaid was managed by a separate commission made up of legislators. The state supreme court has since ruled it unconstitutional for legislators to serve on such executive boards and Mississippi governors now have authority to appoint a Medicaid director.

Welfare

Two weeks before his inauguration, Winter was told by the U.S. Department of Health and Human Services that Mississippi had one of the highest welfare error rates in the country. The state was about to be penalized for inadequate administration of the food stamp and AFDC programs.

Winter was looking for a strong administrator when he recruited Dr. Donald Roark to run the state's Department of Public Welfare. A former Mississippian, Roark was an official of the world's largest farm-credit bank, the Federal Intermediate Credit Bank in Kentucky, but was eager to move back to his home state. Again, Winter delegated heavily to Roark, who used hard-nosed management procedures to reorganize the department and improve staff morale.

Soon after becoming governor, Winter realized that none of Mississippi's 8 counties had a black county welfare director. Since Winter had final approval of county directors named by the State Commission of Welfare, he made it a priority to find good directors who were black. By the time Winter left office in 1984, nearly a dozen black county welfare directors had been hired.

But welfare reform clearly was not a major priority for Winter. Other than his regular monthly meetings with Roark, Winter's chief involvement was to give the director his backing and encouragement, then get out of the way.

"There was very little input from the governor's office," Roark said. Welfare "was a hot potato and nobody wanted anything to do with it." And New Federalism put more heat on the department with substantial cuts in federal assistance for welfare programs.

Early on, Roark restored the credibility of the department's accounting system. After being persuaded that high error rates were linked to low staff pay, Winter publicly supported a substantial salary increase for social service workers. Bigger paychecks improved morale, Roark said, and Mississippi's error rates in AFDC and food stamp programs dropped significantly.

Winter approved the mechanisms Roark needed to redistribute functions of the welfare department. The state began to contract out services to agencies that could deliver better and less expensive services. Mississippi's Council on Aging, for instance, was hired to run the Meals on Wheels program. The move decreased the workload of overburdened state employees and further improved morale.

Winter said New Federalism policies gave governors near total authority over how to spend community development block grant funds. Winter chose to work with county and local governments to create jobs and keep people off welfare. He formed a council to represent all the vested interests, including mayors who had become accustomed to using block grants for public works and neighborhood projects. The council then decided where federal funds could best be spent. In one case, for instance, a faltering industry was propped up and 1,400 people in a single community were kept working.

"There was no way I was going to get a tax increase to expand human services in the welfare area," Winter said. "In fact, we were just doing our best to hold our own on that front."

Summary

Winter, of all the governors studied, comes closest to the James McGregor Burns model of transformational leaders, "who respond to fundamental human needs and wants, hopes and expectations, and who may transcend and even seek to reconstruct the political system, rather than simply to operate within it."[5] He was willing to go out in front to try to create a new value system. At a time when it seemed impossible to accomplish anything, Winter accomplished major reform of Mississippi's schools and educational values.

Tactically, Winter used a vast array of weapons, from paid media campaigns to constitutional change, from coalition building to high political drama. To focus his efforts and his state's resources, he was willing to set priorities and live by them.

The story of Kosciusko, Mississippi, illustrates Winter's ability to transcend limited resources. A bus-manufacturing plant that was the lifeblood of the town closed, laying off about 2,000 employees. Former congressman Frank Smith, a historian and member of Winter's staff, remembered that Kosciusko was the only city in the United States named after Thaddeus Kosciusko, a Polish general who fought for the colonists in the Revolutionary War. Since the 200th anniversary of the battle in which Kosciusko was the hero was approaching, Winter pressed the town to declare a Polish-American day. There wasn't a single Polish-American living in Kosciusko, but busloads came from many cities across the country.

"Out of that experiment, and local pride and local resources—in this case being only the name of the community, . . . totally unrelated to the ethnic background of anyone in the city—there came a local initiative," said Winter. "It tended to focus the attention of the people of that community on their own strengths and resources. Although it was not going to serve a major role in job creation, it did serve, in that particular instance, in getting the heads of a lot of people who were down, up, and looking at the prospects of what they could do for themselves."

Educational reform was Winter's hallmark. He was perplexed by the problems of health care delivery and admitted that he took no great initiatives to reform welfare programs. He delegated to department heads the authority to respond to the opportunities of New Federalism and bring about incremental change. He did not have the time to become personally involved and he was by nature a delegator. He hired competent people.

Winter, constitutionally limited to one term, had only a moment in history. He lost a 1984 bid for the U.S. Senate to incumbent Republican Thad Cochran.

> The greatest frustration I felt was knowing all these needs out there that were unmet and were going to continue to be unmet after I left office, simply because we didn't have the resources," said Winter. "That is always going to be a problem in a state like Mississippi."

Notes

1. Neal R. Peirce and Jerry Hagstrom, *The Book of America: Inside Fifty States Today* (New York: W.W. Norton & Company, 1983), 470.

2. Lewis H. Smith and Robert S. Herren, "Mississippi," in *Reagan and the States*, ed. Richard P. Nathan, Fred C. Doolittle, and Associates (Princeton, NJ: Princeton University Press, 1987), 213.

3. Ferrel Guillory, "William F. Winter: Mississippi's Elder Statesman Preaches the Gospel of Economic Reform," *Governing*, (February 1988): 36.

4. Guillory, "William T. Winter," 39.

5. James MacGregor Burns, *The Power to Lead* (New York: Simon and Schuster, 1984), 16.

3

Texas[1]

MARK W. WHITE, JR., DEMOCRAT, 1983-1987

Context

Some would call Texas a nation unto itself that exerts more influence on Washington than the other way around. Its more than 600,000 square miles and nearly 16 million residents make it a force to be reckoned with. Its power and diversity were evident in 1988, when it produced both Republican presidential candidate George Bush and Democratic vice presidential candidate Lloyd Bentsen.

In 1983, however, when Mark White became governor, the state was in the midst of trying times. "To be a farmer or rancher in Texas during the period," said one observer, "sucked."

The Lone Star state's population grew rapidly in the 1970s because of the rise in oil prices. By 1980, Texas had become the corporate center of the oil industry for the entire world, but it also remained world renowned for its sprawling cattle ranches. The benefits of rapid development were unevenly distributed, leaving a wide range of incomes and living standards. Very little of the black gold's glitter fell on the dirt poor of the Rio Grande Valley or the shanty town barrios of Houston or Dallas.

In the early 1980s, 12 percent of the state's population was black and 21 percent was Hispanic. With almost no unions—Texas is the largest state with a right-to-work law—most minority group residents fall into the low-wage category.

In 1980, Texas was 18th among the 50 states in per capita income but 6th from the bottom in government expenditures per person. Its per capita expenditures for health and hospitals ranked 30th; for education, 31st; and for public welfare, 46th.[2]

Texas's overall tax structure for both state and local government relies primarily on sales taxes, property taxes, and oil and gas severance taxes. The state, itself, has no property or income tax.

The governor has very little power. There is no cabinet. Most actual governing is done by more than 200 boards with overlapping six-year terms. An argument could be made that the lieutenant governor has more power than the governor because he presides over the Senate. He and the House speaker appoint all legislative committees and chairpersons and assign all bills to them. Indeed, White would have accomplished little during his term had it not been for his ability to forge alliances on school reform and public health with Lieutenant Governor Bill Hobby and House Speaker Gib Lewis.

The philosophy of the Democrats who controlled Texas government for most of the post World War II period was to relegate government to the background and let the economy grow by itself. In Congress, however, Democrats Sam Rayburn and Lyndon Johnson led efforts to get federal protection for the oil industry, which was vulnerable to cheaper foreign competition.

The strength of the Democrats weakened as high-income, urban voters became more Republican. William Clements spent $7 million in 1978 to become the first Republican governor of Texas in 100 years. But by the time of his 1982 reelection bid, oil prices had begun to drop. Wealthy urbanites blamed Reagan's economic policies, which Clements supported, for initially failing to turn around the Texas economy. Many stayed home on election day and White, with support from minorities, ousted the incumbent. Clements, however, rode a Texas Republican resurgence back into office in a 1986 rematch.

Profile

Born in Henderson, Texas, in 1940, White earned business and law degrees from Baylor University. He was appointed secretary of state under Governor Dolph Briscoe in 1973 and was elected attorney general in 1978 over James Baker, who would go on to become George Bush's campaign manager and U.S. secretary of state.

White came up in politics as a southern-style Democrat, though he was not as conservative as many of his peers. He would serve many roles as governor, including catalyst, consensus builder, team player and reluctant follower. In a weak-governor system, White was forced to rely primarily on his veto over the budget and his ability to use the bully pulpit. As governor, he was considered short on ideology and long on common sense—competent, but not driven by any desire to reform Texas politics.

White's four-year term was anything but quiet. In the beginning, White thought Texas could afford new initiatives because of a large surplus. Though vague on specifics, he had campaigned with suggestions of far-reaching commitments to education, health and, to a lesser extent, welfare policy. He was rudely awakened, however, when the surplus proved illusory.

Education

A 1982 campaign promise to raise teachers' salaries had won candidate White the active support of teachers and their organizations. The effort to keep that promise ultimately would generate a whole package of important education initiatives. The promise had come naturally to White. His mother, wife, and sister were all schoolteachers and he saw education as central to efforts to resolve a host of serious economic and social problems.

"Much of the remainder of government spending on prisons, welfare and the health services can, in the long term, be reduced by enhancement of our educational system," he said. He argued that improving education was essential to attracting new businesses, especially in high-tech areas.

After his election, however, White learned that Texas no longer had a budget surplus, but in fact, would have a several-billion-dollar deficit his first year in office. He had a promise to keep, but that would be difficult given the politics of the legislature and the economy of the state. Still, he proposed a 24 percent increase in teachers' salaries and a related assortment of sin taxes to pay for it. Despite a television ad campaign, the 1983 legislature refused to pass a salary increase.

In a compromise of sorts, White reluctantly joined Hobby and Lewis to launch an in-depth study of education. White hesitated because he felt the issue already had been studied to death. The legislature approved the study, however, and White, in what proved to be a master stroke, appointed conservative Republican businessman Ross Perot to chair the new select committee on public education.

"We had to capture the national concern for education if we wanted to surmount our budget problems and help teachers," White said. "There was no way that teachers could get a salary increase without a link to broader accountability issues and the growing public concern, stimulated by national reports, for the status of public education in Texas."

What started out as a campaign promise limited to salaries had evolved into a crusade to improve Taxes education.

White wisely relegated himself to the role of just another commission member. He let Perot run the show. When Perot talked about education being in trouble in Texas, the legislature listened. Perot "created interest," White said. "He was a lightning rod. He was convinced that fundamental reform was required and that his group, if it succeeded, would lead the state out of the wilderness."

The commission recommended a $1 billion package of ideas to improve the educational system. Major provisions included development of minimum salaries for teachers and a career-ladder salary supplement; mandatory student-teacher ratios; development of new equalization and school-aid formulas; and creation of the Legislative Education Board to oversee implementation of legislatively defined policies.

The two most controversial recommendations, however, were no pass/no play and teacher testing. In Texas, high school football is as important as God, motherhood, and steak. So the committee's recommendation that acceptable grades—'C' or better—be required for participation in all extracurricular activities, including sports, was considered traitorous.

"All hell broke loose," said White. "Every coach viewed the proposals as threatening their livelihood and the viability of their communities."

A similar furor greeted the notion of mandatory competency testing for all new and existing teachers. Committee members agreed that teacher salaries were abysmally low in Texas, but they were not impressed with teacher standards either. They realized that legislators would have to be convinced of teacher competency before they would approve a pay hike. Three out of four teachers' groups were insulted by even the suggestion of testing. Their opposition, however, proved no match for Perot's ability to marshal the business community and media to his side.

By the time White called a special legislative session in June 1984, educational reform had become the centerpiece of his administration. The lieutenant governor and House speaker successfully resisted considerable pressure from all but one of the teachers' unions and held their votes in line. Perot delivered the support of the business community.

White, Hobby, and Lewis then virtually assured passage of the educational reform package by linking it to a popular proposed increase in highway funding. Even though a relatively small portion of the gas tax in Texas goes for schools, White and his colleagues let it be known that no gas tax bill would be considered until educational needs were addressed by the legislature. While highway advocates were upset, they got the message: Either the educational legislation passes or no highway money. Texas got education reform.

Health [3]

Problems concerning health care for the poor were as immense as Texas. During his campaign for governor, White indicated to Hispanic and black communities that medical indigence was an important issue, but he made no specific promises. He accused the Texas legislature of being stingy and unwilling to spend state funds to secure the maximum amount of federal Medicaid funds.

Just after the election, White joined the lieutenant governor and the speaker to tour the Rio Grande Valley along the Mexican border. They found deplorable conditions, which fueled White's desire to improve all social services, especially health care.

About the same time, a federal judge was threatening to combine several pending lawsuits over health care into a class action and force Texas counties to take more responsibility for meeting indigent health care needs. The state's 254 counties had principal responsibility for the medically indigent, but the state constitution failed to define the counties' role and provided few guidelines. Practices varied from county to county; county contributions were unpredictable; the system was chaotic.

The rapid downturn in the economy, brought on by the drop in oil prices, made White reluctant to initiate any major health programs, despite his earlier desire to help the counties. Besides, he already was committed to raising teacher salaries. With a budget deficit to make up, the 1983 legislature was in no mood for major money bills.

In September 1983, the White-Hobby-Lewis coalition appointed a 71-member task force on the medically indigent, chaired by Helen Farabee, a prominent state senator's wife who had gained visibility in her own right as a respected civic leader. Like Perot, Farabee had prestige and was a respected leader. Hobby was the prime mover on the task force, but White endorsed it. He helped keep the problems of the medically indigent on the political front burner.

"Every time you have the three top officials, including the governor, working together," White said, "it becomes clear to people that this is a major policy issue and that it has some potential or very significant effect on the state."

The task force had four issues on its agenda: the scope of services to be provided; the eligibility criteria governing receipt of assistance; the administrative structure; and the methods of financing indigent health care. Subcommittees assigned to each issue held hearings to gain public and media attention and to gather information for the entire group.

The task force concluded that Texas needed to define and support a clearer, more effective, efficient, and equitable pattern of services. Farabee and the executive committee reconciled most of the disputes between rural and urban counties and between counties and hospital districts. All interests were given an opportunity to make their concerns known. Under Farabee's direction, the committee gradually reached consensus. Meanwhile, White kept his distance, encouraging the task force to proceed but not promising to support any specific proposal.

The group's eventual recommendations focused on mental health, preventive care, and maternal and child health. The package of proposed changes also extended Medicaid coverage to indigent children up to the age of 18. Most significant, however, was a recommendation that defined the role of counties, public hospitals, and hospital districts in caring for the medically indigent. Counties were expected, at a minimum, to take responsibility for people who met AFDC Medicaid financial eligibility standards. But after a county had spent 10 percent of its revenue on the medically indigent, the task force concluded, the state should pick up the rest of tab.

The $120 million package was presented to the 1985 legislature. On the heels of the costly new education reforms, White steadfastly refused to seek any new taxes. Toward the end of the session, he threatened to veto an 8 percent cigarette tax that had been offered to fund the health program. Instead, White proposed scaling back the program to $70 million and funding it from existing general revenue, the governor's contingency fund and various other crannies in the state budget.

Unfortunately, the governor was late getting his proposed compromise to the legislature, and time ran out. Under pressure from Hispanic groups and task force members, White called a special session, during which Speaker Lewis finally broke a tie to pass the scaled-down package.

The bill did not specify a clear-cut source of revenue. Although the legislature debated several alternatives, including a tax on hospitals, none garnered real support. In the end, the governor funded the initial year of the program largely out of his own office budget. The investment apparently paid off. White subsequently touted the Texas indigent health care legislation as a model for other states. Funding has since become part of the regular budget process.

Welfare

Texas is not, never has been, and probably never will be a state known for its receptivity to welfare and welfare recipients. Its AFDC contributions are among the lowest in the nation and support for social services is not extensive.

White placed great trust in the economy's ability to provide jobs. If welfare was provided, it should primarily go to the deserving poor or the poor who could not work. "If a person could work," he said, "welfare should be conditioned on his or her making a serious attempt to work."

Although welfare reform was not a personal priority, White again teamed up with the lieutenant governor and the speaker to persuade the legislature to increase AFDC payments from $32 to $57 per week for a family of four. It was his only major initiative in the welfare arena. Change in welfare policy had no powerful client group and the governor was unwilling to use his limited capital to build support. Even if he had been willing, however, there is no strong evidence he could have succeeded.

Summary

White, despite weak institutional powers and a distressed economy, was able to generate change. He leveraged his own influence by working with the legislative leadership and making inspired task force appointments.

"Even if you didn't like White, his presence helped create an environment in which many important things occurred," said one of the state's leading editors. "Sometimes he resisted, sometimes he led. He viewed change through a political microscope and his priorities were not always clear, but without him, it is unlikely that much of what happened re education, welfare, and health reforms would have happened. . . . He was good copy and had an impact."

Clearly, White's top priority was education. In health, he was a follower and a facilitator. In welfare, he made modest changes, but he was unwilling to invest his personal political resources to build support external to the legislature.

White's leadership style seemed to change from issue to issue. When he cared about an issue, his involvement made a difference. When he cared little, his unwillingness to get involved or to use the trappings of his office helped preserve the status quo.

Notes

1. Ms. Elaine McDade of Austin, Texas provided useful background material for the chapter on Texas. Additionally, Professor David Warner, of the Lyndon B. Johnson School of Public Affairs at the University of Texas, contributed useful material, particularly with respect to health policy in Texas.

The authors also appreciate the assistance of Ms. June Karp, liaison to the Senate committees in Texas, as well as to Ms. Toti Villaneuva, a student at the Lyndon B. Johnson school, and to Ms. Laurie Crumpton, a research assistant to Professor David Warner.

2. Neal R. Peirce and Jerry Hagstrom, *The Book of America: Inside Fifty States Today* (New York: W.W. Norton & Company, 1983), 632.

3. Dr. David Warner and Ms. Augusta B. Villueva of the LBJ School of Public Policy at the University of Texas, Austin, helped secure background data and analyses for the health section of the case study.

4

South Dakota

WILLIAM JANKLOW, REPUBLICAN, 1979-1987

Context

Only 700,000 residents are spread over South Dakota's 99,000 square miles. Seven percent of the 1982 population lived on the state's nine Indian reservations. Despite recreational and hunting opportunities along the Missouri River and the tourist potential of the Badlands and Black Hills, there was little to attract new residents. Until the 1980s, when large corporations such as IBM, Citicorp, Control Data, and 3M began moving in, South Dakota was unable to capitalize on its position near the top of national ratings for favorable business climate.

South Dakota was populated mostly by homesteaders after the gold rush of the 1870s. The new immigrants of northern European descent were attracted by offers of free land. Small towns popped up overnight as rail lines marched across the state. Native Americans were pushed onto reservations, where they did what the white government told them for 100 years.

Politically, South Dakota is dominated by Republicans with a historical mistrust of new government programs. But voter unhappiness with Eisenhower farm policies sent Democrat George McGovern to Congress in 1956 and to the U.S. Senate in 1962.

Democrats continued to ride the wave of unrest that swept the country during the Vietnam and Watergate years. In 1970, Richard Kneip became the second Democratic governor of South Dakota in 50 years. The same year, the state constitution was amended to extend the governor's term from two to four years. Kneip was reelected in 1972 and the Democrats gained control of the legislature. However, McGovern, who won that year's Democratic presidential nomination, failed to carry his home state against Richard Nixon.

South Dakota's Republican Party, in debt and disarray, was looking for new leadership when William Janklow appeared on the political horizon. Janklow, who was elected attorney general of the state in 1974, was viewed as young, aggressive, and feisty. He participated in and, some have said, led the state's response to the American Indian Movement's sometimes tension-filled campaign for Indian rights in South Dakota.

The division between whites and Native Americans was one major issue during Janklow's years as governor. Additional problems came from the 1982 rural recession that had been several years in the making. In the 1970s, despite declining farm income, banks made agricultural loans based on highly inflated land values. When land values plunged in the early 1980s, farmers and ranchers, whose wealth had been built on paper, experienced losses similar to the 1929 stock market crash.

With no personal or corporate income tax, South Dakota relies on a sales tax for most general-fund revenue. The rural recession meant reduced tax revenue. Local governments, facing a rural backlash against rising property taxes, looked to the state for more aid, especially in education. Limited resources constrained state activities during the Janklow administration.

Profile

Janklow was born on 13 September 1939, in Chicago. He moved to South Dakota while in grade school after the death of his Jewish father, a prosecutor at Nuremberg. Growing up in the eastern South Dakota farm town of Flandreau, Janklow became a self-described juvenile delinquent who never finished high school. Under pressure from a judge, he enlisted in the Marines one month before his 17th birthday. He returned some years later to South Dakota where he talked his way into the University of South Dakota and eventually earned a law degree.

Janklow spent seven years as a legal services lawyer on the Rosebud Indian Reservation. He said the experience gave him an intense awareness of and commitment to Indian issues. But later, as assistant attorney general, Janklow was chief prosecutor of state charges stemming from a riot at Custer that involved AIM. Running on the Republican ticket in 1974, a generally Democratic year, he was elected attorney general as a champion of law and order. A year later, when Janklow appeared at an AIM encampment outside Oglala after two FBI agents were shot and killed, he accused the Bureau of Indian Affairs of allowing the AIM suspects to get away. By this time, Native American activists and their support groups were calling Janklow racist.

With his reputation as a tough-talking, gun-toting attorney general well established, Janklow won 57 percent of the vote when he was elected governor in 1978. Republicans also regained control of the legislature. During his eight-year administration, Janklow coped with the double dilemma of declining federal grants and a reeling rural economy. He pushed, forced, threatened, cajoled, and browbeat just about everyone until his programs were adopted. He quickly dominated the part-time lawmakers and used the power of the budget office to run virtually a one-man show.

Higher education administrators found Janklow meant business when he delivered on his threat to withhold their budget requests from the legislature until they agreed to a unified accounting system. All the colleges and universities in South Dakota now use the same accounting system.

Ironically, Democrat Kneip installed the strong-governor system that gave Janklow his tight-fisted control of state government. Kneip got bipartisan support from the legislature to eliminate scores of boards, commissions, and advisory groups that had ruled over departments and offices. The centralization of power significantly increased the authority of the governor.

Bill Janklow's instincts and proposals both anticipated and preempted the regulatory aspect of the new federal-state balance brought on by New Federalism. Despite increased flexibility to administer human service programs, Janklow couldn't get enough deregulation. He said the regulatory climate in Washington was a constant frustration.

On the budget-cutting side of New Federalism, Janklow and his Republican-dominated legislature readily accepted provisions of the federal Omnibus Budget Reconciliation Act of 1981, which reduced or froze block grants and entitlements. "We used the 1981 budget cuts to cut what otherwise couldn't be cut," Janklow said.

The "Renaissance in Federalism" proposal Janklow sent to Washington went a step further by proposing that South Dakota receive one federal check. He and his people suggested that they were willing to take less money if federal funds could be coordinated and managed in a flexible manner. The proposal was rejected, despite what Janklow called "the rhetoric of the Reagan people."

Janklow admits he never went through the process of determining objectives and setting priorities. His initiatives were "piecemeal." While some governing was "budgetarily driven, a lot of it was just trying to identify problem areas," he said. "One method was to just go out and identify program areas and try and deal with them until they were cleaned up."

His central theme was making the best use of the resources available and not raising taxes.

Education

Three years of attending National Governors' Association conferences convinced Janklow he needed to flag education as a major issue. He used both the real and symbolic power of the governor's office and his Republican Party leadership to keep pressure on lawmakers to support educational initiatives. State aid to K-12 education increased by approximately $8 million per year during the eight years of Janklow's administration.

Before proposing specific initiatives, Janklow delegated the job of gathering basic data about K-12 schools to Diana Miller, his chief of staff and a former head of the South Dakota Teachers Union. Janklow said he mistrusted Scholastic Aptitude Test (SAT) scores, which ranked South Dakota in the top three states nationwide, because only the students who planned to go to college took the tests.

Miller looked at such things as dropout rates, curricula, and what percent of students went to college. Her six-month study concluded that students in larger communities were driving up statewide averages on test results and graduation rates, while rural schools were producing few stellar students. Few rural high schools had teachers who specialized in more technical subjects such as science or math.

"When I finally got all the information, I wanted to puke," Janklow said. "The perception that we had a great education system in South Dakota was just baloney. So I'm in the position of going in (to rural school districts) and telling them, 'look you've all got cancer' when they all felt pretty good about themselves."

Still, Janklow never developed a fixed plan for pervasive and long-lasting change in the education system. Instead, a continuing dialogue with educators, lawmakers, and cabinet members kept education initiatives coming. They ran the gamut: mandatory availability of kindergarten, vouchers for interschool transfers, consolidation of rural schools, curriculum improvements, vocational-technical program expansion, student skill testing, and teacher advancement certification.

Janklow was especially aggressive in pushing consolidation of small rural high schools. He believed it was necessary because of changing demographics. As people moved to urban areas, a number of rural high schools had dwindled to 20 or 30 students. The trend both impaired the quality of education and was costly to the state.

Janklow's lobbying for legislation to enable consolidation was so personal that one cabinet member recalled "legislators being lined up to go in to talk to the governor one by one." Legislation was approved with little fanfare. It allowed the state to pay a local district full tuition of up to $3,600 the first year for every student sent to a new school because of a merger. The state would pay one-half the tuition the second and third years.

Teachers supported consolidation because they generally were sympathetic to weeding out marginal schools and teachers. Janklow had built what he called a "reservoir of trust" with teachers by featuring education as a campaign issue, making education a personal priority, and involving teachers in his initiatives. Now he used them as a constituency group to counter formidable opposition to consolidation.

Janklow worked to convince the Municipal League and Chambers of Commerce that their communities would survive if students were bused to merged high schools. He tried to assuage local school boards' and community officials' fears that students would be unable to compete in many programs if they were in larger schools. Janklow was only half joking when he said the biggest mistake he made while promoting consolidation was not making it illegal to eliminate a basketball team.

During Janklow's administration, schools were closed in 34 of the state's 201 school districts. Janklow said the vast majority of the mergers occurred in the northeast quadrant of the state, where there is a small town about every eight miles.

Janklow, while later regretting the time and effort invested, reverted to his dictatorial style in getting legislative approval of a form of teacher certification. Teachers feared local school boards would use certification as an excuse to keep salaries low. School boards argued it took away their local control.

"I just rammed it through," said Janklow. "I fought it and fought it and fought it and fought it until I got it passed. I was more of a dictator when I was governor. People would accuse me of that every day and I'd say, 'Yes, but I'm benevolent.'"

Janklow captured the media's undivided attention by making a special address to the legislature. He proposed that each teacher be accountable to a certification committee composed of representatives from the employer school, the college that issued the teacher's diploma, and the state Department of Education. Janklow personally attended legislative committee meetings to refute testimony against his plan. On Saturday mornings, he went to "eggs and issues" sessions lawmakers held in their home districts.

"I was successful, but there were better things I could have gone to the mat on," Janklow said. "One should not have to burn their political capital on a fire that is only going to burn so small. The end result is everybody is still certified anyhow. I was looking for a method to provide a substantial increase in salaries that would be tied to some performance criteria."

Health

Janklow's major health care initiative was called the Indian Health Care Improvement proposal. It was successful only in opening precedent-setting communication with tribes, medical schools, state health officials, and federal overseers of the reservations.

The plan called for increasing the physician faculty at the University of South Dakota's School of Medicine to provide primary and specialty care services to individual reservations. To support the physicians, Janklow's staff proposed adding ancillary staff, increasing clinic space and equipment, improving air and ground transportation systems, and establishing a more advanced communications system.

The disparity between the health status of Native Americans and whites had been long recognized. Janklow was the first to bring all the interested parties to the table, but he didn't involve the tribes soon enough. The plan was not tendered to the tribes for approval until after it had been developed within the administration. No "ownership" by local interests had been built. And since the federal government had jurisdiction over reservations, the request for money would have to go to Washington, D.C. The tribes, perhaps remembering Janklow's anti-Indian reputation during the AIM heyday, were unwilling to form a coalition with the governor. The funding request never got further than the Indian Health Service.

Janklow blamed the federal bureaucracy for adding to the state's other health burdens by failing to control medical costs. He said South Dakota had no problems with simple homes for the elderly until federal mandates required that they be converted to full-blown nursing homes. They had to be equipped with skilled nurses, patient councils, social activities directors, and "God knows what else."

Medicaid costs skyrocketed, even though there was no demand for the rapidly increasing supply of hospital and nursing home beds.

"We had no history in South Dakota of senior abuse," he said. "The homes were really places where old people went so they weren't homeless when they couldn't take care of themselves. They weren't really sick."

Janklow got some control over hospital costs by calling attention to exorbitant local fee schedules. He contracted with the Mayo Clinic in Minnesota to take South Dakota's indigent care cases. When state medical centers complained, he threatened to tell South Dakotans with ability to pay that it was cheaper to go to Mayo.

Janklow also imposed what amounted to a moratorium on certificates of need for additional health care facilities. He said the system for determining need before increasing capacity failed because every request was granted.

"I wasn't able to beat the certificate of need system but . . . I ordered the state secretary of health not to approve any more," he said. Applicants eventually gave up trying to make it through the Janklow-imposed bureaucratic process.

Additional savings came from moving developmentally disabled patients from two state institutions into group homes. Janklow obtained a federal waiver allowing Medicaid funds to be used to care for and train clients in a community setting. From 1978 to 1986, the population at Redfield State Hospital and School dropped from 843 to 351.

"It cost us a lot more money to keep them in a hospital than it did to put them in a group center," he said. And with physical and social therapy programs, the patients' quality of life improved. "I think the more freedom and the more things that the people can do and learn, the better off they are."

When the legislature balked at moving the developmentally disabled into group homes, Janklow mobilized his kitchen cabinet, the budget office, and his own powers of persuasion. He personally lobbied the Republican caucus and worked with the Association for Retarded Citizens to lobby the appropriations committee. The legislature backed away from its go-slow approach and eventually supported community-based programs in the budget process. No enabling legislation was required.

Janklow lamented the lack of support from the medical community when he tried to expand a program for nurse practitioners in rural areas. Janklow wanted to staff old hospitals and clinics—"some better described as first aid stations"—with nurse practitioners under supervision of private physicians who could be many miles away.

Doctors resisted. "They are frankly so selfish, and you don't realize it," said Janklow. "They have the toughest time deciding on anything."

Janklow instead put physicians directly on the state payroll to monitor more than 1,500 practitioners scattered throughout western South Dakota. "It's become a very sufficient, politically very strong, very successful program," he said.

Welfare

Janklow showed his flair for the dramatic when, shortly after his inaugural, he taped together all the required welfare forms and applications and rolled an 85-foot long scroll down the Capitol steps. It was his way of serving notice that modernizing the state's welfare program would be a priority.

The Automated Eligibility System finally was implemented in 1985. It would not have happened without Janklow's command that the Department of Social Services "do it." The computer-based program automatically determines eligibility for Aid to Families with Dependent Children and food stamp applicants and recipients. While South Dakota's AFDC error rate already was low, AES helped reduce instances of agency error to the lowest in the nation and eliminated some avenues of fraud.

Although the clergy protested, requiring welfare recipients to perform public service work appealed to South Dakota's conservative legislature. Janklow proposed a welfare program that excluded women from work requirements if they had small children. He insisted that all other able-bodied welfare recipients work for at least 20 hours a week or attend vocational rehabilitation programs. The legislature adopted Janklow's recommendation in 1980. One year later, South Dakota became a demonstration state for two federal programs—Work Incentive and Community Work Experience.

Janklow sidestepped or ignored federal regulations when they impeded his effort to cut the numbers and length of stay of children in foster care. One such rule prohibited continued federal assistance to foster parents who decided to adopt foster children.

"Someone in Washington had decided that this was a mechanism that they would use to prevent people from getting to the head of the line on adoptions," he said. "With special-needs children it made absolutely no sense. There are no waiting lines to adopt a child that has Down's syndrome or cerebral palsy, yet foster parents would get these kids, fall in love with them and not want to let them go, and we were prohibited from allowing them to be adopted."

Janklow ignored the rule and used the foster program to promote special-needs adoptions. The state no longer could make cash payments once an adoption took place, but children were kept on Medicaid to help the families meet medical costs.

Janklow also bent the rules to allow AFDC-eligible families, a group including many Indian families, to adopt children.

"They had everything good going for themselves other than the fact that they had no wealth," Janklow said. "We would let them adopt a child and the child would go on as a natural child on the AFDC roll and become part of their monthly AFDC program."

Janklow disdained federal programs he believed made a welfare class out of people who lived their entire lives on low incomes but did not think of themselves as poor. The elderly on Social Security and Medicare especially resented being called welfare recipients.

Janklow told the federal government what it could do with vast quantities of commodity cheese when the feds didn't like South Dakota's method of distributing it. Senior citizen groups had been told they were violating health regulations when they cut down five-pound boxes of cheese into more manageable chunks. Janklow ignored the regulations and the warnings. Eventually, the federal government quit threatening to stop the program.

"It took me about four years to figure out that I could really ignore a lot of the federal rules and wouldn't have to face the sanctions," he said. "I finally hit upon what I felt was the Bronx defense. Nobody ever made the Bronx pay anything back . . . in the history of the U.S. Frankly, I just started ignoring all the federal rules and it made a remarkable difference in our ability to do things."

Summary

"Ramrod" may be the most polite way to describe Bill Janklow's role as governor. Janklow himself admits to having been "probably more of a dictator, a browbeater." Other descriptions include heavy-handed or "bully." What's often missed, however, is the versatility that let the South Dakotan move from catalyst to power broker. He marshaled every available resource to reach a goal.

Perhaps no one but a Janklow could have pulled off closing one of the state's seven colleges and turning it into a prison. South Dakotans for years had debated the need for seven state-supported colleges in a low-population state. Janklow decided he could address the problem of prison overcrowding and reduce money spent on higher education at the same time.

"It was the toughest fight I ever had," he said. While his kitchen cabinet assisted in negotiations and his budget office created options, Janklow personally lobbied for citizen support. He traveled to Springfield several times to discuss the proposed campus closing. He also formed strategic alliances with the House and Senate majority leaders.

Janklow used the "bully pulpit" to marshal public opinion and kept lawmakers well informed. After bitter debate, the legislature narrowly voted to close the Springfield campus and convert it into a prison for about 400 inmates. Academic and vocational programs are available for inmates who earn their way there from more secured prisons.

Cabinet members said the fight to close the Springfield campus took the greatest toll on Janklow both personally and politically. During his last year as governor, observers said, Janklow appeared listless, burned out and frustrated.

Janklow was a hands-on governor whose absolute control sometimes meant selective attention. His most pressing issues became the state's most pressing issues. He concedes that his personal involvement may have caused him to sometimes "lose sight of the big picture." He acknowledges lacking the patience needed to build constituencies that would lead to long-term and permanent changes.

While Republicans welcomed Janklow's firebrand style in the beginning, his one-man rule did not win him many friends in the legislature. In 1986, the Republican-dominated appropriations committee turned on him and rejected most of his proposals. They may have been angered by Janklow's decision to force incumbent U.S. Senator James Abdnor into a primary campaign.

Janklow was prohibited constitutionally from seeking a third term as governor. After losing to Abdnor (who in turn lost to Democrat Thomas Daschle in the general election), Janklow first joined a public finance firm, then practiced law, expressing no desire to return to elective politics.

5

Colorado

RICHARD D. LAMM, DEMOCRAT, 1975-1987

Context

Colorado was booming when Richard Lamm was elected governor in 1974. By 1980, the census would show 2.88 million residents, up 31 percent from 1970. The Rocky Mountains lured new residents with opportunities for jobs, recreation, or adventure. Nineteenth century miners struck it rich with gold and silver; 20th century miners were attracted by the prospect of producing synthetic fuels from the vast oil shale deposits on the Western Slope.

Ever a concern is water, which is vital to farms and ranches as well as the cities of the Front Range, the 300-mile strip that separates the mountains from the plains and supports about 80 percent of the state's population. Every Colorado governor since territorial times has had to wrestle with the problem of how to get water, how to store it, and how to allocate it to downstream states on both sides of the Continental Divide.

The Colorado settlers of the 1970s, however, generally had little interest in such mundane matters as water, education, and care for the aging. They were young, mostly single or newly married professionals. They were caught up in global environmentalism, disarmament, and getting rid of corrupt government officials in the wake of Watergate. Lamm was one of the crop of Democrats swept into office by the 1974 post-Watergate backlash.

Growth had not yet reached its peak in January 1975, when Lamm was inaugurated for the first of his three terms. Denver's skyline was punctuated with building cranes as new office towers were built in anticipation of energy development. Fortunes were made in residential and commercial real estate.

New Federalism hit in the middle of Lamm's second term, when change was already under way in Colorado. Republicans had regained

49

control of the legislature. The economy, largely due to a drop in oil prices, was beginning to falter.

"The longer I went into my term, the less money there was and the more creative my managers had to be in stretching limited resources," Lamm said. His priorities changed from "learning to divide a growing pie to making the pie grow again."

By the time Lamm left office in 1987, the bottom had fallen out of the energy market. Oil shale development on the Western Slope had collapsed. The disappearance of high-paying jobs in the energy industry left many families among the working poor. Empty office buildings in downtown Denver stood as silent monuments to the speculative boom of the early 1980s. By 1986, more people were moving out of Colorado than in.

The legislature, in the meantime, returned to its historically conservative ways under the leadership of the so-called "House crazies." They were elected in 1976, when Democrats lost control of the House. These rookie Republican lawmakers were conservative to the brink of radicalism. By 1984, Republicans had a big enough majority to override the Democratic governor's vetoes.

Profile

Dick Lamm was born in 1935 in Madison, Wisconsin. He had earned a bachelor's degree in business, a law degree, served two years in the army and been certified as a public accountant before moving to Colorado. He immersed himself in Democratic politics and was elected to the House of Representatives for the first of four terms in 1966. He became governor at 39.

Lamm is typical of the new Coloradan. He is bright, reads voraciously, and loves to backpack and climb mountains. He sponsored the 1967 bill that gave Colorado one of the most liberal abortion laws in the country. Citing environmental concerns and the lack of financial accountability, Lamm led the 1972 grassroots movement that persuaded voters to reject a plan for Colorado to host the 1976 Winter Olympics.

In his later years as governor, Lamm became an expert on contemporary political and economic issues. A misquote that had Lamm saying the elderly had a "duty to die and get out of the way," although later corrected, thrust him into the national spotlight as a critic of health care spending priorities. His pessimistic view of the future won him the moniker "Governor Gloom."

Lamm's critics argue that his success as governor was compromised by his enduring inability to forge an effective working alliance with the legislature. A keen debater, Lamm could be feisty and combative with opponents, most often Republican lawmakers he viewed as obstructionist and reactionary. Some speculated Lamm's third-term preoccupation with national and international issues grew out of his frustrations with the Colorado General Assembly.

Lamm often rejected advice that he do more to court his opponents. He was not a backslapping politician; he preferred think tanks to cocktail parties. "Besides," he said, "I was raising a family in the governor's mansion. I wasn't prepared to take on the legislature, two at a time, and invite them over to dinner and schmooze them every night. It was just not my style."

In addition to his personal and partisan differences with the legislature, Lamm believed there was an enduring tension between the executive and legislative branches of government. While he said he regretted not getting along better with his legislature, he also suggested that governors and legislatures may be natural adversaries, no matter what their political persuasion.

Under Colorado's weak-governor system, Lamm had very little formal control over the state budget. Even the ability to set the legislature's "short session" agenda was taken from the governor by constitutional amendment in 1984.

Lamm frequently, but with infrequent success, turned to the bully pulpit and constituent coalitions in efforts to override the legislature. Although he had persuaded voters to veto funding the Winter Olympics, he was not able to convince them to pass a minerals severance tax. And despite his strong opposition, voters twice approved a ban on public expenditures for abortions. Lamm also was frustrated in his quest for higher user fees on commercial trucks and more controls on the transportation of hazardous wastes. He was out of office before the legislature eventually adopted such measures, at least in concept.

One of the few powers Lamm had was to direct the flow of federal funds coming into Colorado. Since the block grants of New Federalism had few strings attached, the Republican-dominated legislature tried to restrict the governor's authority to allocate federal dollars. The effort died amid arguments that Colorado wouldn't always have a Democratic governor.

Lamm, a delegator, said he believes his most important contribution was to give Colorado "a good management team who managed the state honestly and well." The team improved the efficiency of state government. But Lamm admitted that many marginal programs were cut more for reasons of budget necessity than philosophical intent.

Lamm never sought dollar-for-dollar replacement of reduced federal allocations as welfare eligibility criteria were tightened by the Reagan administration. For one thing, Lamm was a realist and didn't expect any money bills to get through the tight-fisted legislature. Lawmakers already were striving to balance the budget amid declining revenue. For another, Lamm was also fiscally conservative and more inclined to cut spending through greater efficiency than to raise taxes to increase revenue.

Only in the last two of Lamm's twelve years in office did he actively pursue economic development. Until then, he viewed his job as handling "this incredible growth that was coming at us."

Education

There was no effective constituent pressure to change Colorado's educational system during Lamm's 12-year tenure. Even if there had been, there was little the governor could do. The independently elected state board of education appoints the state's commissioner of education. Furthermore, school reform in Colorado, Lamm observed, would have to be initiated by local school districts.

This "almost monomaniacal belief in education as a local issue," Lamm said, may have been why Colorado failed to develop a critical mass to change state education policies. But change also was hampered by a general perception that the education system wasn't all that bad.

"Colorado was not near as backward as Mississippi was," Lamm said. "When your state is last or second to last, it's always easier to whip people up. Our school people would keep patting us on the head and saying everything is fine." Still, Lamm gave Colorado a 'D-' for its lack of interest in reform.

One of Lamm's few personal successes in education came with the 1985 "second chance" program. The enabling legislation passed only after Lamm formed an unlikely alliance with conservative state Senator Steve Durham, a charter member of the "House crazies." The program gives returning high school dropouts a chance to pick which schools they will attend, regardless of residency requirements. Durham was attracted by the idea of introducing market forces and competition into the public education arena.

The governor played a more limited role in passage of the Educational Quality Act of 1985. The program initially was funded by withholding from each district an amount equal to $3.70 per pupil each year. The additional revenue paid for evaluation testing, gifted student programs, dropout prevention efforts, and teacher career ladder programs. Lamm publicly supported the bill, directed his lobbyists to push it, and signed it. But his chief contribution may have been keeping restive Democrats from rebelling against any measure that cut state aid to schools.

Lamm was perpetually thwarted in his struggle to restructure the distribution of state aid to local school districts. About 50 percent of Colorado's K-12 funding came from the state under a formula based on local districts' ability to raise revenue through local property taxes. Since assessed valuations varied widely, so did state aid allocations.

After the state supreme court came within one vote of finding the system discriminatory, Lamm made school-finance reform a priority. He stressed the need to change the distribution formula in nearly every State of the State message, and in 1983, he enlisted John Fuhr, his Republican opponent in the 1982 general election, to join him in chairing a task force for excellence in education.

Even with bipartisan leadership, however, the project led nowhere. The task force recommendation for evaluating teachers was seen by teachers' associations as an attack on tenure. Legislators found the proposed increase in state support to be too expensive. Inaction was also blamed on Lamm's generally antagonistic relations with the General Assembly. Most important, however, may have been Lamm's failure to build a coalition, to convince Colorado voters their schools were in trouble.

Colorado's School Finance Act wasn't revamped until a year after Lamm left office. The Public School Finance Act of 1988 promised a minimum of $68.78 per pupil in state aid and phased in additional state aid to districts with low assessed valuations of property. Lamm dismissed the measure as a Band-Aid, claiming the legislature made only the minimum change necessary to avoid massive court-ordered reform.

Health

Ironically, the one area for which Lamm would become best known nationally, health care, was the one in which he was least knowledgeable when he became governor. Eventually he identified health as a key issue, then set the priorities and policies that would become the trademark of his administration. He relied heavily, however, on cabinet members and staff to innovate and implement.

"When I went into office, I didn't know anything about health care," he said. "I'd never worked in the area. I'd never carried any bills in the area. It was way late in my term before I knew the difference between Medicare and Medicaid."

By the time he left office, he was convinced that runaway health care costs—driven in part by doctors' fears of malpractice suits and by the proliferation of high-cost, high-tech procedures—were sapping the nation's strength.

Lamm initially was forced to study cost-containment strategies because the cost of medical care was rising at twice the rate of inflation. Public assistance caseloads soared as the economy slipped into recession. But because of revenue shortfalls, the legislature consistently underfunded Medicaid. The groundwork for cost containment was laid by a 1983 task force convened by the governor and staffed by his office. A later cabinet council, consisting of cabinet officers of all departments concerned with health care services, was directed to implement the recommendations of the task force.

At Lamm's urging, the legislature created a Health Data Commission in 1985 to gather correct information on health care costs. As one of the biggest customers of health care services, the state was able to use the commission's data to make better purchasing decisions. The same information was passed along to the public and forced providers to become more competitive and efficient.

Among the strategies used to squeeze fat out of the system and contain Medicaid costs were reviews of admissions to and use of hospitals and nursing homes; computer analysis of pharmacy use; development of alternatives to nursing home placement; and Medicaid payments based on stipulated fee schedules, which had been put out to bid, rather than billed charges.

"In the health care system, there was enough money spent that we really did have some flexibility to reorganize and give more service for less money," Lamm said.

A coalition of health care purchasers helped Lamm diffuse providers' opposition to his cost-cutting measures. Doctors, hospitals, and nursing home operators were outmaneuvered by coalition members, including the state and private businesses, who collectively spent more than $500 million annually on health care.

Like many states during the period, Colorado sought and received federal permission to move many developmentally disabled patients into less restrictive and less costly community facilities. Federal courts and Congress were forcing the states to adhere to new standards for the care of developmentally disabled persons. Simply warehousing them in institutions would not do.

Lamm took the initiative to reduce the population at the state hospital in Pueblo from more than 1,100 patients to about 50. Most patients were moved into 28 group homes, which had been built during Lamm's tenure with money from federal block grants. As state jobs were eliminated in Pueblo, Lamm sought to find dislocated workers new jobs in alternative care facilities.

While the local media and legislators from the economically depressed Pueblo area objected to deinstitutionalization, Lamm had little trouble finding bipartisan support for his measures. He also had rare authority to decide how the money from federal block grants would be spent.

"Most of us very much supported the idea that we could take less money for more flexibility," said Lamm. "When the rhetoric stopped and all of a sudden we had to get in there and allocate some of these block grants, God, it was miserable."

Lamm's views on health promotion and fitness were a natural extension of his deeply held belief that each person ultimately is responsible for his or her own health and well-being. He created programs to emphasize physical fitness. One governor's council sponsored annual sports events. And by executive order, Lamm banned smoking in all state buildings in 1984.

Welfare

As a fiscally conservative Democrat, Lamm often concerned himself more with the budgetary than the social impacts of welfare programs. He more often focused on efficiency than on equity issues. He was skeptical of programs that he believed fostered dependency rather than employment and independence.

Lamm's philosophy is seen in a foster care program that, between 1979 and 1986, reduced the number of children in foster care by 20 percent. Lamm believed counties could be given greater flexibility in developing and implementing programs to keep troubled children in their homes. He pushed legislation creating a Placement Alternative Commission in each of Colorado's 63 counties. The state provided start-up money for new programs, but capped foster-care allocations to the counties. Counties provided a variety of support services to parents that were less expensive than foster care placement.

Lamm also pressured county welfare agencies to do a better job of verifying welfare eligibility. The state literally took over management of Denver's food stamp program because the error rate was so high.

"I went down to the Denver welfare office that had incredible abuses. It was simply an inefficient system; a very sleepy, inefficient place," Lamm said. "I had to go meet twice with [Mayor] Bill McNichols to kick his people in the butt to get going and do some of these things."

Lamm, to the chagrin of his own Democratic Party, refused to veto a bill removing Colorado from participation in the AFDC-UP program, which gave aid to families with dependent children when two parents were in the home but the primary wage earner was unemployed. The legislature's decision ended assistance to about 1,200 families.

Calculating that a veto would be overridden, Lamm chose instead to mobilize his cabinet and leverage the Job Training Partnership Act to find jobs for those no longer eligible for benefits. Lamm instructed every department from highways to education to look for jobs and training opportunities for the wage earners in affected families.

A similar Jobs Strategy program gave AFDC applicants a choice between a job and public assistance. A series of bills adopted by the 1986 legislature required each county to find ways to give work-ready recipients a job instead of a welfare check. Lamm provided clear direction for the program, held news conferences to explain it to the public, lobbied the legislature to pass it, and forced interdepartmental cooperation to implement it.

Another priority for Lamm was enforcing court orders for child support payments. County-by-county collections were increased, but Lamm said more could have been done through a centralized state collection agency. The idea failed to pass the legislature, he said, because the district attorneys, while not paying much attention to child-support collections, did not want to relinquish jurisdiction to a state agency.

Summary

Despite 12 years in office, Lamm never would be able to claim authorship of exciting innovations in education and human services. Except for cost containment, he was not ideologically disposed to go out in front to change the health and welfare system. His persistent warning of the need for school finance reform went largely unheeded.

In retrospect, Lamm said Colorado could and should have done a better job stepping into the vacuum left by the reduction of federal welfare programs.

"In Colorado, we met that challenge in our typical legislative way," he said. "We shifted it on to another level of government. I think one reason Colorado is 47th in state taxes and fifth in local taxes is that our Legislature did not meet the challenge."

New Federalism forced a shotgun marriage between Lamm's drive to make the best use of resources and the legislature's desire to save money. The unlikely union led to one of the nation's most aggressive efforts to contain health care and welfare costs. Lamm's role was to study and identify key issues, set priorities, articulate the general policy direction, then rely on his appointees and the bureaucracy to implement programs.

Lamm was a shrewd tactician and manager, but was hampered by the weak powers Colorado accords its governors. And because of his adversarial relationship with the legislature, he had very little opportunity to lead Colorado in new policy directions. Rare successes occurred only when Lamm's fiscally conservative instincts dovetailed with legislators' inherent reluctance to spend.

Lamm was one of the more studious and intellectual politicians to become a governor. As a futurist, Lamm was the first nationally prominent politician to tackle the thorny issue of biomedical ethics. Despite repeated attempts to lure him back into politics, Lamm seems to have found a permanent niche as an expositor of contemporary national political-economic issues.

6

Vermont

RICHARD SNELLING, REPUBLICAN, 1977-1985

Context

Vermont, the nation's second most rural state, works hard to keep from becoming the East's ultimate suburb. It walks the line between sustaining enough growth to keep the economy moving and preventing development from spoiling the quiet lifestyle and pastoral environment for its nearly 600,000 residents. As early as 1970, Vermont was forced to pass tough new land-use restrictions to slow development. Farmers were unable to pay property tax bills because land values had been driven up by wealthy urbanites' demand for ski condos and summer homes.

The state's population is largely homogeneous. Only 0.2 percent of the residents are black. The main contrast is between rural Yankee congregationalism and the Catholic-ethnic makeup of the cities. One-fifth of Vermont's citizens live in Burlington.

Though historically considered one of the most Republican states in the country, Vermont had Democratic governors through most of the 1960s and 1970s, and socialist Bernard Sanders was Burlington's mayor from 1981 to 1989. Until the 1980s, Vermont's legislature was dominated by Republicans, but voters seem to be wary of conservative positions on social issues. Independent John Anderson did well in Vermont in 1980, when Ronald Reagan carried the state with only 44 percent of the vote.

Vermont is one of only three states to elect its governor every two years. The lieutenant governor is elected separately. The state has a tradition of enacting the governor's budget unless there are strong arguments from the opposition. Governors have the power to put in place many key state officials.

State government is strong in Vermont. Because there are no counties, the state provides many public services. Taxes are relatively high.

A progressive tradition of using government resources to improve the human condition has prevailed since the early 20th century.

Snelling, a progressive Republican, struggled to provide both efficient government and adequate human services. For the first two of his four terms, he managed a prosperous state. Revenue surpluses led to tax cuts and there was low unemployment. Vermont didn't escape the recession of 1982, but by the time Snelling left office in 1985, Vermont again was experiencing growth and tax revenue, was rebounding.

After steering Vermont through the ups and downs of the economic cycle, Snelling persuaded the state to adopt a "full cycle" fiscal policy. In good times, he said, the state should hold expenditures to not more than 2 percent above the rate of inflation and give the rest back in tax reductions. In bad times, Vermont should go into debt to maintain critical programs and wait until the economy recovers to retire the deficit and consider a new round of tax relief. But to the Governor's enduring disappointment, his successor did not follow through on the plan, which had been supported during his tenure in office.

Profile

Snelling was born in 1927 and raised in Pennsylvania. He was an infantry private during World War II and graduated cum laude from Harvard University in 1948. He moved to Vermont and founded Shelburne Industries, which manufactures ski racks and other accessories. He ran unsuccessfully for lieutenant governor in 1964 and for governor in 1966. After serving three terms in the Vermont House of Representatives, he was elected to his first of four terms as governor in 1976.

Snelling's friends call him direct and candid; others have said he could be brusque and abrasive. No one disputes his honesty and sincerity.

As a successful businessman, Snelling was a devotee of the "plan-sell-implement" model, in which planning is done rather quickly and efficiently by insiders, technical and substantive experts, and executive branch officials. When applying the model as governor, Snelling identified problems and structured solutions. He then tried to build the coalitions and support needed to push policies and programs through to implementation.

The model often requires a tough sell because important interest groups are left out of the planning process. The stakeholders may not trust the planners, particularly if they are "government" planners, and may believe they have as much expertise and information as the experts who developed the plan. Implementation may become difficult or impossible, as Snelling discovered with his Cost Control Council's 1977 recommendation that the state-owned Weeks School be closed and the property sold.

The Weeks School, a juvenile reformatory at Vergennes, was beset with problems. The 80 inmates were an unhealthy mix of underage people convicted of crimes, including murder, and other juveniles who had merely been adjudged unmanageable. Runaways were common.

The U.S. Department of Labor's 1978 offer to lease the school as a Job Corps federal training center appeared to be a workable alternative to selling the property. Snelling initiated the idea and communicated to his cabinet that it was one of his top priorities. The state, presumably, would find alternative placement for individuals assigned to Weeks.

Closing the Weeks facility met with immediate criticism. Several penal officials claimed they had not been sufficiently involved in the planning process. They indicated that precise strategies had not been thought out for alternative programs to accommodate the school's "hardcore" repeat offenders. According to Snelling staffers, penal experts who criticized the plan favored an institutional, more traditional approach to incarcerating juveniles. They did not like the fact that some Weeks inmates would be, and indeed were, placed in foster care, while more serious offenders went into a minimum security facility called the Benson Wilderness Camp.

After a legislative inquiry and continued criticism from the media and neighbors of the Benson facility, the Snelling administration responded with an option. A portion of the revenue Snelling raised by leasing Weeks went into building a 20-bed, maximum security detention facility. Still, Snelling declared the program "very successful."

Though viewed as somewhat conservative within Vermont, Snelling was considered moderate in the outside world. He was chairman of the National Governors' Association from 1982 to 1983. Even as a Republican governor, he was among the most vocal critics of New Federalism as promulgated by President Reagan.

"We have a tradition in America of taking care of those less fortunate than ourselves," he said. "America must address the questions of what resources do we have, where are they, and how can we employ them fully in order to come as close as we can to meeting the national sense of a standard of decency. I thought New Federalism would attack this, but it was not on the administration's agenda."

Despite his disappointment in the Reagan agenda, Snelling found the New Federalism agenda useful in his quest for a more efficient and economic way to run Vermont's human service and education programs. The block grants were tailor-made for the technocratic Snelling. The opportunity to coordinate programs and presumably secure a better allocation of resources, he said, was "one of the reasons it's worthwhile being Vermont's governor."

Education

Snelling knew a lot about education before he took office. His mother and wife both had started private schools and his daughter was an assistant to Education Secretary T.H. Bell. A strong task force on education gave him information during his first campaign for governor.

Nevertheless, Snelling later said a failure of his administration was his inability to reform school finances, despite three increases in state aid to K-12 education in his eight-year tenure. Mere increases, he said, didn't address the variance between different communities' ability to ante up the rest. Indeed, average annual family income ranged from $45,000 in some counties to $13,000 in others.

True to form, Snelling relied on the technocrat's plan-sell-implement method to reform school financing. After a rigorous analysis of policy alternatives, he selected a preferred option.

"My conclusion was that we needed a statewide property tax on non-residential property to go to a state aid-to-education," he said.

In 1979, he went public with a proposal for a state tax on nonresidential property and a reappraisal of all assessed valuations. It would have raised $66 million to increase the state's contribution to K-12 education and equalize per-pupil expenditures among the counties.

When Snelling tried to sell the proposal, however, a panoply of interest groups arrayed themselves against him. Local governments and school districts, while welcoming the prospect of more state aid and a revised distribution formula, uniformly argued that a state-imposed tax on nonresidential property encroached on the exclusive revenue source of local governments—the property tax. The legislature agreed.

Snelling said his proposal didn't sell because he failed to recognize how strong the objection to the loss of local control would be. "This fundamental principle of local control of local assessments," he said, was violated by his plan. "One can not advocate something which has a known disadvantage without recognizing the disadvantage," he said. "I was a broken record. Had the statewide property tax succeeded, I would have claimed it to be perhaps the most important thing I did for education."

Snelling had some small successes in education that required no legislation. He used his control over block grants from the Labor Department to launch an all-out attack on illiteracy through the Department of Employment Training. He also started governor-sponsored institutes in art and drama, science, and the liberal arts. He involved business and industry in another institute that identified skills sought by the private sector and contracted with schools to provide them.

Health

Vermont has long had a tradition of concern for public health and a strong medical program for the needy. It was the first state in the country, more than 130 years ago, to make it illegal to inquire how a hospital bill would be paid before admitting the patient. Vermont has a low infant mortality rate; its citizens live longer than the national average; and it has a high ratio of physicians to population.

Because of the strength of its medically indigent program, Vermont had little trouble maintaining services after federal Medicaid cutbacks. But as Snelling began seeing health care costs rise faster than inflation, he looked for ways to prevent health problems that government would otherwise be expected to address. He used his authority to spend federal block grants, once they were accepted by a legislative committee, to fund some of the suggested solutions.

"Our effort was to design new preventive programs which deal with, and reduce causes," he said. "Unless you find ways to deal with causes, you will probably find it difficult for a health department to keep up with the task that will be presented."

Snelling's staff concluded after analysis that alcohol abuse was a common denominator in the problems of health, crime, and joblessness. One program was developed with federal funds to counsel and treat expectant mothers who had alcohol-abuse problems. It helped reduce the need for postnatal care of their newborn infants.

Snelling also turned to the Labor Department for block grants to identify and solve health problems that prevented clients from holding jobs. Again, Snelling said, alcohol was found to be a pervasive cause. Implementation of treatment programs for the alcoholic or malnourished was assigned to staff.

When it came to containing hospital costs, Snelling understandably had difficulty building support within the hospital lobby. The so-called "maxicap" on hospital charges was the most important and controversial recommendation from the Vermont Commission on Health Care Costs, which Snelling created in 1982. Snelling had confidence in the commission and accepted the recommendation the plan to put a maximum limit on hospital charges.

Vermont's 16 hospitals were outraged. Other health care providers joined them in lobbying the legislature to protect their freedom to determine charges. Snelling, the commission, and insurance companies pressured the legislature to adopt the "maxicap." The governor, his staff, and the commission took the issue to the media and major purchasers of health care, including insurance companies. Still, the legislature took a middle ground. It created a Hospital Data Council and endowed it with limited authority to review hospital budgets and make its findings public.

Snelling accepted the council as a compromise that would ultimately "lay the foundation for a future maxicap." The president of the Vermont Hospital Association, however, labeled even the compromise "garbage." Snelling may have lost the battle but he appeared to have won the war. The Hospital Data Council, through the powers of publicity, has been able to slow the escalation of hospital costs.

Welfare

Snelling's approach to welfare was shaped by another campaign task force before he took office. It included developing common application forms for human services and reprogramming computers to eliminate double and triple dippers. Snelling's philosophy was to meet immediate human service needs but at the same time determine where the needs came from and intercede where possible.

At Snelling's instruction, coordinating panels of cabinet officers met twice a week to work on health and welfare programs. Snelling delegated implementation to three cabinet officers. One was his secretary of human services: the president of a Catholic college, a nun, and a Democrat who had chaired the campaign for Snelling's opponent in the 1976 campaign. Another was the head of a preelection task force on human services who became his secretary of administration. The third was an attorney who had been a state welfare commissioner and who became Snelling's legal counsel. In all the welfare programs, Snelling, the manager, promoted and facilitated coordination among the departments.

"We spent a great deal of time in the first three or four months of my administration deciding what the plan of action was," said Snelling. His cabinet members "knew the game plan and they executed."

Welfare clients were treated individually with the goal of getting them off welfare. If the core problem was alcohol or a chronic illness, treatment programs were made available. Literacy and training programs were set up for the unemployed who needed them. Federal block grants again provided the needed funds.

The AFDC-UP program, which provides assistance to two-parent families when the primary wage earner is unemployed, was pinpointed as an area of potential savings. New AFDC-UP applicants who were found to have acceptable job skills were put on a fast track through the employment and training system.

Snelling set up a troika to avoid any infighting or turf protection among the three directors of the agencies involved in AFDC-UP, making all three jointly responsible for the success of the program. They met regularly to focus on ways to move primary wage earners into training and employment as quickly as possible. The unusual approach got significant results. Vermont's Department of Human Services reported that the AFDC-UP caseload dropped by 70 to 80 percent.

The Vermont Futures program grew out of the 1982 recession and cast Snelling in the unfamiliar role of a welfare liberal. The machine-tool industry in the Springfield area was especially hard hit—unemployment reached 12 percent—but Snelling was convinced the downturn in the economy was temporary.

"Conservative Republican that I am, I immediately thought of the WPA," Snelling joked. He was serious, however, in proposing that the state develop public works projects for the temporarily unemployed. He added the condition that each project have a public benefit and add more value than it cost. Snelling argued for the program during his morning coffee with legislators in his statehouse office. Only after a sustained and determined lobbying effort by Snelling's staff and cabinet did the legislature narrowly approve it.

"There was a great deal of travail in the state at the time," Snelling said. "Unemployment was high. There were all kinds of reasons why people wanted to help, so that made it easier."

Vermont Futures was financed with a $5 million general obligation bond issue. Between May 1983 and December 1984, 1,000 people were put to work on 86 projects, ranging from repairing roofs at the Capitol to building salt barns for the highway department.

"My only enemies were my conservative Republicans," Snelling said. "After years as majority leader, I would have been seriously disappointed if they hadn't attacked me. It was one of the ways I gained consensus."

Snelling delegated more in the area of welfare than he did in health or education, but he didn't give up any responsibility for the final product.

"Delegation is no excuse for mismanagement," he said.

Summary

Just as Snelling's skills as a planner-coordinator brought him the major successes of his term, so the failure to successfully involve constituencies and build diverse coalitions—as in the "maxicap" episode—led lead to some of his biggest disappointments.

Snelling is credited with being one of the most effective technocratic and managerial governors of the '80s. His prescription for effective government includes agenda-setting—"the prime task of any chief executive"—and "the hard work of analyzing what you think is wrong."

The plan-sell-implement model worked well in the arena of transactional politics. When sufficient power and resources reside with the governor, this approach to change can work. It is especially effective when there is broad-based public support, as in the Vermont Futures program. Snelling sometimes augmented his formal powers by reminding legislators of his statewide constituency.

The planner-managerial method is less effective, however, when preliminary fact-finding is inadequate, when sufficient time is not allowed for planning, or when empowered interests or stakeholders are lined up against an issue or program. Snelling might have won on the hospital "maxicap" proposal or school finance reform had he been more able to convey the need to constituent groups.

"You're talking about people saying 'yes' or 'no,'" Snelling said of his successes and failures. "Until they say 'yes' or 'no,' there can be no change."

7

Idaho

JOHN EVANS, DEMOCRAT, IDAHO, 1977-1987

Context

It is doubtful that John Evans foresaw the problems the next decade would bring when he became Idaho's governor in 1977. With a diversified economy based on agriculture, mining, forestry, and recreation, Idaho had experienced years of steady but modest economic growth. The state's legislature in the 1970s was predominantly Republican, but had a rapport with popular Democratic Governor Cecil Andrus. When President Jimmy Carter named Andrus interior secretary, Evans was elevated from lieutenant governor. He had every reason to be optimistic.

The bottom began dropping out of Idaho's economy in 1979, shortly after Evans was elected to his first full term. The farm economy showed serious signs of a slump. A national energy crisis began cutting into mining and timber revenue. Cleanup and emergency agricultural relief from the 1980 Mount St. Helen's disaster was expensive. A damaging riot at the state prison took another big chunk from the relatively small budget of a rural state. Unemployment rose; federal revenue sharing fell. Evans was forced to put the brakes on all state programs and cuts were felt across the board.

"We didn't have the luxury of having many programs that other states have—that you could identify—that you could eliminate," he said.

Idaho is mostly rural. Only 5 of 44 counties contain urban centers, and they are small ones at that. The population of nearly one million residents is predominantly white. The 1980 census showed that only 3 percent of Idaho's residents were Hispanic, 1 percent Asian American, and 1 percent Native American. With about 25 percent of the people claiming affiliation with the Church of Jesus Christ of Latter Day Saints, Mormons dominated both the state's culture and politics.

Idaho relies heavily on its governor as chief executive and author of the state budget. Evans's life as governor was made more difficult by the policies of New Federalism. To the governor, the policy seemed to provide more responsibilities and less money to the states. With Idaho facing the largest state budget deficit in its history, Evans pushed his initiatives against mounting economic woes and increased opposition from a Republican legislature. Evans easily won reelection in 1982, but the legislature became more conservative, reflecting the politics and philosophy of President Reagan. By the last two years of his tenure, Evans had to deal with a veto-proof legislature.

Profile

John Evans was born in 1925 to a ranching family in rural southwestern Idaho. He served in the U.S. Army in World War II, then returned to Idaho to engage in ranching and banking.

Evans had paid his political dues when he took over as governor. He was elected to the Idaho Senate in 1953 and spent 14 years in the legislature. He demonstrated statewide appeal by winning a three-way Democratic primary for lieutenant governor and a general election race against a strong Republican in 1973.

Evans is a Mormon. But unlike Allen Larsen, his Republican opponent in the 1978 governor's race, he did not attempt to mix the Mormon religion and view of morality into his political agenda. Evans later would use his knowledge of Mormon values to try to liberalize attitudes toward welfare and public health by emphasizing family-centered services.

As revenue became more scarce and the philosophical gap between Evans and the legislature widened, Evans became more aggressive, frank, and direct. Critics said he had a temper that sometimes got him into trouble with legislative leadership. Supporters note that he faced a very partisan, conservative legislature. To some, Evans seemed unwilling to negotiate with legislators, preferring instead to bring grassroots pressure to bear. Said one former GOP leader: "He seemed to use the stick without the carrot." Evans's staff members, however, said he did what he had to do to sustain commitments.

Evans believed he had to seek additional tax revenue to keep needed programs. "We still had to provide for children, education, and health for seniors and children," he said. When the legislature balked at raising taxes, Evans sought the help of groups interested in specific social programs that would be cut. He appointed their members to task forces. He used social-welfare constituencies to persuade—some would say pressure—the legislature to approve incremental sales tax increases that eventually totalled 2.5 percent.

"Bringing in task forces was a strategy that you had to use against a very conservative legislature," Evans said. "We had to go out and mobilize the people first."

Evans knew he couldn't change the legislature's dominant philosophy, so he attempted to change the political environment. He claimed small victories whenever he wrung more money out of the legislature.

Education

Idaho was making curriculum changes before the 1983 federal publication *A Nation at Risk* spotlighted the need for improving education systems across the states. Evans built a consensus by capitalizing on a perception that the Idaho system needed help. The Idaho Education Association (IEA) was solidly behind him.

"Idaho was the Mississippi of the West," he said. "We had the lowest of the salaries and the lowest contribution to the educational system."

Evans found and appointed members to the state board of education who would assume responsibility for both higher education and public schools. Historically, board members had yielded responsibility for K-12 education to the independently elected superintendent of public instruction. During the Evans years, the superintendent was Republican Jerry Evans, who was elected the same year John Evans was elected to his first full term as governor. They were not related by family or politics, but frequently worked together to promote better education and more state funding for schools.

With its 1984 School Improvement Act, Idaho became one of the first states in the country to require completion of a core curriculum—including science and math—for graduation. John Evans, in his symbolic role as chief executive, supported the act. Most of the curriculum requirements, however, were written by Jerry Evans.

In 1978, Idaho passed a Proposition 13-type initiative, the 1 Percent Amendment, which capped local property taxes. Governor Evans appointed a bipartisan task force to examine the fiscal impacts of limiting property taxes to 1 percent of valuation. Members concluded it would bankrupt many school districts and force 50 percent cuts in local government services. The task force recommended a moratorium on implementing the initiative.

The legislature imposed three one-year moratoriums. However, it also limited local school districts' ability to raise revenue by freezing for two years the amount of funds that could be secured through property tax levies. The third year, school districts could increase property tax revenue by up to 4 percent, as long as the new total did not exceed 1 percent of assessed valuation.

Task force chairman Dr. Sydney Duncombe credited Evans with preventing a disaster in school financing. However, the governor kept quiet about his success because he had substantially reduced the impact of a citizens' initiative. The legislature and Evans never agreed on the level of funding for education. Evans said no real improvement would occur without more money. Lawmakers said Evans consistently wanted too much money.

The Idaho Association of Commerce and Industry, the IEA, and Superintendent Evans sided with Governor Evans. The business group, which argued that more companies would locate in Idaho if the educational system was improved, and Jerry Evans helped win over the Republicans. Over a three-year period, lawmakers reluctantly approved sales tax increases totaling 2.5 percent. The state share of funding for public schools and higher education went from about 45 percent in 1978 to 75 percent in 1987.

Health

The federal Omnibus Budget Reconciliation Act of 1981 forced states to set priorities and make tough choices about health and welfare programs. Idaho was no exception. Evans spent several years lobbying the legislature for more funds to replace lost federal dollars. In most cases, the assembly claimed empty pockets and refused to increase support.

With limited resources, priorities had to be set. Evans directed the state Department of Health and Welfare to identify priority population groups. Among them were chronically mentally ill adults and emotionally disturbed children. Evans had the budget authority to use federal block-grant funds to protect and expand programs for those targeted groups.

The fiscal crisis meant state and local agencies in Idaho were hard-pressed to maintain well-used, but high-cost, rural mental health services. Evans lobbied for adequate program funding and kept legislative committees informed of the urgency of the problems. He never succeeded in getting increased financial support from the legislature. But his direct involvement in shaping Department of Health and Welfare policies was considered key to retaining most rural mental health services.

The governor also worked with state hospitals and community mental health centers to deinstitutionalize the mentally ill into community-based programs. He overcame opposition of community groups by emphasizing the merits of outpatient programs and the need to modern-ize mental health services.

When neighborhood groups tried to use local zoning laws to restrict group homes, Evans rallied support from churches. He appealed to a collective consciousness of caring for the less fortunate. An awakened citizenry helped the governor convince the legislature to pass a law exempting group homes from prohibitive zoning regulations.

As legislators scoured the budget for ways to cut, Evans's caretaker role took hold. He used another citizens' task force to block the disman-tling of Idaho's system of regional health centers and programs. The task force evaluated the cost-effectiveness of such a move and convinced the legislature that it would cost more to eliminate the regional pro-grams than to keep them. The programs were saved.

The Evans' administration again used the grassroots strategy to win funding for a statewide Emergency Medical Services program. It required little arm-twisting, however. Everyone from county commis-sioners to the medical community to rural lawmakers saw the need for isolated mountainous regions to be part of a statewide network to pro-vide emergency medical care.

By matching federal block-grant funds, the state helped needy com-munities purchase ambulances and other emergency medical equip-ment. The state also provided financial assistance to counties, which were responsible for the care of the indigent and of trauma victims. An uncoordinated, rudimentary emergency medical service was converted into a statewide system linked by mountaintop microwave transmitters.

Evans took a particularly proactive stance on health issues related to children and the elderly. As a result of a children's conference he held early in his administration, Evans formed a Division of Children and Children's Health in the Department of Health and Welfare. He and his staff were adept at mobilizing children's advocate groups when the leg-islature was reluctant to support child-oriented health programs. In this context, the Children's Trust Fund was created by the legislature in 1985. In two years, about $92,000 was raised through a taxpayers' checkoff program. One beneficiary, respite care services, gave parents a break by placing their disabled children in a protective environment for a period of time. A number of shelters and child development programs also were funded by the trust.

Idaho's well-organized senior citizens were a strong constituency for Evans. They urged the governor to do everything he could to help them stay in their own homes.

"Senior citizens feared more than anything else having to face the real-ity of having to go to a nursing home," Evans said. He spoke at a 1979 conference of the Senior Citizens Council and launched "Operation Independence." Working with the council and medical industry representatives, Evans helped stem the flow of seniors into nursing homes. Meals on Wheels and other in-home services proliferated. They helped reduce the demand for Medicaid and other federal government programs, which became increasingly scarce during the Reagan years.

Welfare

As the federal government backed out of or reduced welfare programs, Evans looked for ways Idaho could take up the slack despite hard state economic times. He moved cautiously to reform welfare policy. He tried to modify the antiwelfare bias of the legislature by focusing attention on expanded family-centered services.

"We are a very strong church state with a dominant population of Catholics and Mormons," Evans said. "Mormons have their own programs; they take care of their own essentially in that process. So they don't have strong needs. The perception is . . . 'why doesn't everybody else take care of their own?'"

Evans believed children from needy families were most vulnerable in hard times. He showed lawmakers firm numbers of child abuse and neglect cases. He lobbied the legislature for many years, all the while promoting the value of the family. He gradually won increased appropriations for family services and child protection to augment the Children's Trust Fund.

Evans faced difficulties in the AFDC area, despite his and his welfare director's repeated attempts to increase AFDC payments. The obstacles were great. For one, AFDC caseloads were increasing because of the recession and higher unemployment. For another, changes in federal policies required increased AFDC support from a state that already had a declining economy.

As the cost of managing the AFDC component in the State Department of Health and Welfare rose, Evans ordered layoffs of state social service employees. Despite this fact, legislators told him he was asking for too much money. Only after Evans pointed out the state's legal responsibility to AFDC recipients did lawmakers approve a supplemental appropriation. But Idaho never was able to maintain welfare payments to those who lost eligibility during the early Reagan years.

With the help of senior citizen and nursing-home groups, Evans successfully lobbied the legislature for supplemental appropriations to address a dramatic increase in Medicaid recipients. The alternative would have been to tighten eligibility requirements and turn away many residents.

"We never viewed our seniors' program as a welfare program," Evans said. "Seniors are the first ones to say they aren't on welfare. To them, supplemental security income is really social security and they aren't on welfare. They think they earned it."

Evans worked hard to create a bipartisan approach to human-services needs. Evans believed he used up considerable political capital with the legislature during the Medicaid and AFDC struggles. He recognized that his successes were limited in the social-welfare and social-services areas. He wished he could have done better.

Summary

John Evans's lasting legacy could be his success in minimizing the effects of the state's fiscal crisis on the delivery of human services programs. When his predecessor, Cecil Andrus, joined the Carter cabinet in 1977, Evans inherited a state with an economy already going downhill. Evans vetoed legislative cutbacks. He used his political skills and popularity with grassroots coalitions to slow down or freeze legislative attempts to dismantle important programs. He returned the state intact when Andrus returned to the statehouse 10 years later.

Evans had to scramble to balance the state budget and maintain essential programs from the time he took office. He improved the efficiency of state government through management changes, but he had little chance to change basic policies, particularly in health and welfare.

The legislature approved a number of sales tax increases during Evans' tenure. The additional revenue increased the state share of public school funding. It is doubtful whether educational funding would have been increased without the support of the Republican superintendent of public instruction.

"It wasn't much fun to be governor when John Evans took over," said Dave Humphrey, Evans's deputy director of the Department of Health and Welfare. "The state had its worst fiscal crisis in history. We had our most conservative legislature that I can recall. There was little room for Governor Evans to make a dramatic policy impact."

Evans emerges as the classic transactional leader—negotiating, accommodating, forming alliances, and brokering to save the programs he saw as important to Idaho. Evans's major contribution was to hold things together. Indeed, the *Idaho Statesman*, the state's largest newspaper, called Evans "the best goalie Idaho has known."[1]

Notes

1. "John Evans Made the Best of Tough Times," *Idaho Statesman*, 4 January 1987, sec. F, p. 2.

8

Wisconsin

LEE DREYFUS, REPUBLICAN, 1979-1983

Context

Stability through diversity could be Wisconsin's theme. While other states approached the 1980s under a growing shadow of recession, Wisconsin enjoyed a comparatively prosperous economy. State government was not called on to dig deep or cut back to address the social issues of education, health, and welfare.

Wisconsin's population grew by 6.5 percent during the 1970s to reach the 1980 census of 4.7 million residents. Wisconsin residents were well educated and stable; 70 percent of residents 18 and older had high school diplomas. Only 8.7 percent were below the poverty level. Sixty-nine percent of those 14 and older had lived in Wisconsin all their lives. With an economic base spread among manufacturing, agriculture, retailing, and tourism, unemployment was well below the national average. Blacks were the state's largest minority, at 4 percent of the population. Blacks are concentrated in urban areas, however, so in most Wisconsin counties, the largest minority is either Native American or Hispanic.

A key to understanding Wisconsin politics lies in the ideology of the Progressive Party. Progressivism was founded in Wisconsin in 1900 by then Republican Robert Marion LaFollette. Preceding the New Dealers of the 1930s, LaFollette believed government, to the extent possible, must help ordinary citizens recover from hard times. Incorporated into progressivism was the "Wisconsin idea" that the concepts of university social scientists could be converted into practical legislation for the good of the people. Wisconsinites have always demanded a high-profile state government and paid high taxes to get it.

Wisconsin politics can not be defined in traditional Democratic or Republican terms. The state that sent LaFollette to the U.S. Senate has since ranged in its choices from the communist-baiting Joseph McCarthy to William Proxmire, the penny-pinching Democrat who made a career out of exposing the "golden fleecers" of government.

Recent gubernatorial elections also demonstrate an inconsistent electorate. Republican Lee Dreyfus was a popular governor who was preoccupied with lowering taxes. When Dreyfus declined to seek reelection, Wisconsinites elected liberal Democrat Anthony Earl. He generally believed that government should be active in expanding people's choices. After one term, Earl was defeated in 1986 by another tax cutter, Republican Tommy Thompson.

"In Wisconsin, where you have a heavy dose of Democrat liberalism," Dreyfus said, "there was always that heavy dose of German socialism, of which I would be typical. You would be socially responsible but fiscally absolutely conservative. Wisconsin has been a state that could always elect socialist mayors in Milwaukee, turn out Joe McCarthy, and have no problem doing both."

During the 1970s, Democrats held virtually all major offices in the state and controlled the legislature. Republican Dreyfus was elected governor in 1978 on a tax-cutting and tax-reform agenda.

A self-styled political "outsider," Dreyfus struck a responsive chord with voters when he promised to reduce a $1 billion budget surplus and return most of it to the taxpayer. "The key initiative for me was tax reform," he said.

Dreyfus, upon becoming governor, had the advantage of strong institutional powers. The governor in Wisconsin appoints the heads of 14 departments, plus the members of numerous commissions, boards, and councils. The governor establishes special committees and task forces by executive order and maintains full authority for budget development.

Profile

Lee Sherman Dreyfus was born in 1926 in Milwaukee. His father was a radio program director and his mother a teacher who became president of the Milwaukee school board. After serving in the U.S. Navy during World War II, Dreyfus chose careers in communications and education, mixing hands-on experience in broadcasting with a fast-track rise in the university world. His communications skills would serve him well during his four-year venture into elected office. Indeed, he viewed his job as governor as that of communicator and salesman.

As chancellor of the University of Wisconsin at Stevens Point, Dreyfus was outgoing and available to students. They recognized him by his ever-present red vest. He took both his red vest and an open-door policy with him to the state Capitol.

Dreyfus was a maverick who appealed to Wisconsin's independent-minded voters. He had never held an elective office before. He had only loose ties to the Republican Party. However, because of his lobbying on behalf of the University of Wisconsin system, he was well traveled and well known politically.

"I got into the political process to reform the tax trends," he said. "I had to join a party in order to run. I ran literally against the party in the primary and then against the incumbent."

The incumbent was Democrat Martin Schreiber, who had become acting governor in 1977 when Governor Patrick Lucey was appointed ambassador to Mexico.

Dreyfus said he would not have objected to increased taxes had people voted for them. But inflation and Wisconsin's progressive tax structure had fueled a "money machine that nobody could shut off." Dreyfus' decision to focus on taxes was his own. "I was appalled at the amount of money coming in."

Dreyfus' upset victories, first in the GOP primary and then over the Democratic incumbent, gave him the clout he needed to push his tax ideas through the legislature. He succeeded his first year in securing legislative support for returning $942 million in taxes to the people. His tax package indexed the income tax so the rate would not go up even though income increased during an inflationary cycle.

By the end of his term, however, the Midwest's deep recession had begun to affect Wisconsin, and the state faced a projected $300 million deficit. Dreyfus proposed a temporary sales tax increase amid rumblings that the legislature was considering raising the state income tax. Dreyfus argued that an income tax increase would institutionalize new revenue surpluses at taxpayers' expense.

Finding little legislative support for his plan, Dreyfus engineered an all-out, take-it-to-the-people campaign. He used his significant communication skills in live television appearances. After one 30-minute TV special, he had cabinet members staffing telephone banks to receive incoming calls. Public sentiment for the governor's proposal was overwhelming and the legislature eventually passed a sales tax increase. A selling point was the stipulation that, once the budget situation eased, the increase would be rescinded or rebated in the form of property tax relief.

Dreyfus maintained an open administration. His "bull pen" office was designed with the desks of major staff officers—including his legal counsel, chief of staff, and press director—literally out in the open. He held weekly news conferences but issued no press releases. Statehouse reporters had their own bench in his office from which they could observe the daily workings of the executive branch.

This concept of open government came from Dreyfus's mother. On one of her frequent visits, while he was a professor at Madison and she was president of the Milwaukee school board, she refused to meet with a group of his colleagues about the problems of racial segregation in the schools. She said she did not discuss public school business in private.

Adopting her principle both as chancellor and governor, Dreyfus said individuals intimidated by his open-door policy were people who "couldn't talk if they couldn't whisper." The only time he closed his office door, he said, was to discuss personnel or political strategy.

Republicans complained Dreyfus seemed to court the Democratic majority in the legislature more than his own party. Dreyfus said he rarely had any contact with any legislative leaders.

"I saw the governorship like the university presidency," he said. "I dealt with the external constituencies and the department chiefs, like university deans, handled internal policy and administration. My Cabinet would deal directly with the legislative leadership on both sides and that made my party mad. I tried to listen to the people. I delegated. I was not a planner or a grand policy person."

Education

Dreyfus inherited a good educational system that fit well with his support of strong local control. He was wary of any notion that Washington, through the Department of Education, was going to "fix" education. He didn't believe he should, either.

Dreyfus said he thought his tendency as a chancellor and professor "to say the governor ought to keep his nose out of the university" kept him from pushing for school-system reforms or changes. Besides, according to Dreyfus, Wisconsin citizens generally felt their schools were providing students with a reasonable education.

However, to encourage more accountability to the taxpayer in K-12 education, Dreyfus moved to make local school boards separate elected bodies with the power to impose taxes independently of city governments. He believed school boards were avoiding responsibility by blaming city councils and town boards for property tax hikes and other education-related problems.

"That whole idea really got played around but didn't take hold," said Dreyfus. "The school people were very ambivalent. One side of them would want their own tax-raising ability but the other side didn't want to give up the protection that city governments afford when the heat is on."

Local politicians also did not want to give up their taxing authority and convinced the legislature to reject Dreyfus's proposal to mandate separately elected school boards. However, Dreyfus won a concession when the legislature required that tax bills clearly state how much tax revenue went for government and how much for schools.

"That took the pressure off local politicians who felt they were getting blamed for what the schools were doing," Dreyfus said.

Dreyfus said the increased sales tax also helped take the pressure off the property tax as a major source of revenue for the schools. While some argued that the sales tax was regressive and forced the poor to pay a greater percentage of their income, Dreyfus noted that clothing was the only taxed necessity. Utilities, gasoline, and food purchased at a grocery store were exempt.

"The shift to the sales tax was popular," he said. "We may see an increase in the sales tax as a way to reduce property taxes. The increase of property taxes is where the tax revolt is growing."

Another improvement Dreyfus sought for Wisconsin's educational system was statewide competency testing for students. A 1980 study showed that 20 percent of the state's residents 18 and older did not have high school diplomas. Dreyfus argued that by identifying a competency problem as early as second grade and repeating tests every two years or so, the schools could give pupils whatever attention they needed to keep them on a track toward graduation.

The proposal faced strong opposition from teachers' unions and other educational factions. A substitute measure that gave school districts a local option of whether or not to test was passed in the omnibus state budget bill. Dreyfus vetoed the provision, hoping the teachers who opposed him would propose a more acceptable proposal for the 1982 legislative session.

"I understood the concern of the Wisconsin Education Association that competency testing would be used as a measure to evaluate the competency of the teacher," he said. He did not want teachers to focus on merely preparing students to take the tests. Nor did he want the best teachers assigned to the worst cases, as superintendents might be inclined to do, to keep test scores up.

Dreyfus said his veto acknowledged WEA's concerns, but he also expected the teachers' union to return with its own proposal for measuring learning increases without measuring teaching. That didn't happen. As a result, when a nearly identical bill for optional student competency testing passed in the 1982 omnibus budget bill, Dreyfus signed it, calling it a "critical first step" in providing students with basic learning skills.

"It was a half-a-loaf reaction in part," he said. "The very groups I had given the opportunity to build something that would really work and be better did not get into gear and do it."

Health

To the chagrin of his own party, Dreyfus retained cabinet member Donald Percy, an appointee of the previous Democratic administration, and gave him more authority. Percy reorganized the Department of Health and Social Services. He centralized planning for greater efficiency. He looked for ways to expand services to client groups.

Dreyfus, the marketer, saw his role as developing the constituency for the deinstitutionalization and cost-cutting initiatives Percy had begun during former Governor Schreiber's administration.

"Wisconsin has, in my opinion, a lot of good government and it's not party-related," he said. "There is a continuum here."

With the second-highest number of nursing-home beds per capita in the nation, Wisconsin was especially hard hit by rising medical costs. Dreyfus claimed the federal government, through Medicaid, was in part responsible for a growing trend of warehousing the elderly to get them out of the way. He imposed moratoriums on approving new hospital and nursing-home beds and granting hospitals' requests for the newest equipment.

Dreyfus, believing community-based programs also would help control medical costs, authorized Percy to design a Community Options Program (COP) to find alternatives to institutionalization. Its purpose was to provide home-care support or community-based assistance wherever possible to avoid commitment to nursing homes. Elderly and disabled clients, working with county administrators, could make their own choices from a varied and flexible menu of long-term support options.

Percy took primary responsibility for designing the program and building support for it. Dreyfus lobbied personally for the program, holding direct discussions with community, legislative and bureaucratic leaders.

The legislature gave COP resounding approval despite objections of county officials who were afraid of hidden costs and joint program administration with the state. Further resistance came from health-care providers and the nursing home industry, whose expansion efforts were thwarted. Dreyfus said he overcame the opposition by concentrating on county-level advocacy groups for the disabled and elderly.

"We tried to go beyond the various advocacy groups at the local level to find the leaders who cared about health care within the community," he said. "They were real people, dealing with real constituents, and knew them by name."

Dreyfus said he inherently mistrusted organizations that claimed to represent statewide special-interest groups. When one group said it spoke for the state's 168,000 veterans, he responded, "Nope, you don't speak for me and I'm a veteran."

Launched in 1981, COP spread to all 72 counties in four years. Although total cost savings were hard to prove, audits showed clients were well served. Handling a case under COP was less expensive than keeping a person in a nursing home under Medicaid.

Dreyfus was also concerned with the excessive costs of high technology and the related competition between hospitals for the latest in technology. "You get a small town with two hospitals and they both want a CAT scanner," the governor said. "It's downright inefficient."

Dreyfus used the certificate-of-need process to restrict the acquisition of expensive new technology. Through this means, he said, he was able to force consolidation of some hospitals. Dreyfus needed no legislative authorization to deny certificates of need. The opposition, led by major health-care providers, never got organized enough to beat him.

"The large operators had the resources for expansion, but I think they decided early on it wasn't worth it to pick me up as an opponent," Dreyfus said. "In fact, in the long run, they knew we had to improve the whole delivery system and they would be hard pressed to go against me."

Dreyfus used his extensive budget authority to put an enrollment cap on the medical school. He said Wisconsin had no shortage of doctors, only uneven distribution, and could not afford expensive education for medical students who then moved out of state.

There was little opposition to the enrollment cap. The medical community, however, soundly rejected Dreyfus's proposal to give free medical school education to students who would agree to practice for five years at a location chosen by the state. The plan was seen as a form of indentured slavery. It never developed into a formal proposal to the legislature.

Welfare

Dreyfus's welfare initiatives were not very far-reaching. He felt that tax reform, in many ways, was welfare reform. Raising income tax brackets to reflect inflation removed the lower income levels from tax liability. "We removed a pile of people from taxes," Dreyfus said.

According to Dreyfus, the expanded sales tax also protected the poor. "There was no sales tax on food, except food you get in a restaurant; no sales tax on energy and electricity during the winter months," he said. "There was no sales tax on any kind of prescribed drugs."

Dreyfus supported very narrowly focused welfare reform. The approach was developed by Percy under Governor Schreiber in 1978. But it became a Dreyfus initiative and he signed it into law his first year as governor. It emphasized family responsibility through stringent child-support collections and encouraged self-sufficiency through job incentives.

"I set the groundwork and began to create a constituency for the notion that, by God, women shouldn't have to keep begging the court to make their ex-husbands do what they should do," Dreyfus said. Now Wisconsin supplements living expenses for children if their fathers can't pay support.

Dreyfus made aggressive use of federal block grants, which he had authority to spend, to support private employers who hired AFDC recipients. Unlike workfare, which assigned public-sector jobs in exchange for welfare, Wisconsin's jobfare program gave monetary support to private employers.

"If you hired the poor, then the state would provide part of the base which meant the corporations could hire these people for a very cheap rate," Dreyfus said.

A 1979 fuel assistance grant program exemplified the governor's hands-off approach to dealing with the legislature. He articulated his concern that the poor and elderly would be unable to pay fuel bills because of rising gasoline prices and escalating home heating fuel costs. But he left it to the legislators to develop the actual fuel assistance plan.

The governor's office worked with the Democratic legislative leadership for swift adoption of a county-administered fuel assistance grant to eligible households. The state spent nearly $4.5 million in emergency assistance during the early winter months of 1979. Federal grant money later became available through a program Dreyfus advocated as vice chairman of the Committee on Energy and Environment of the National Governors' Association.

Dreyfus ran interference for Percy's welfare initiatives by cutting through bureaucratic red tape, even traveling to Washington, D.C., when necessary. He lauded the increased flexibility that came with New Federalism because it "gave Wisconsin a very real opportunity to begin to do some of the things we wanted to do."

In general, Dreyfus followed Percy's lead on most health and welfare programs. The governor believed his key function in the welfare arena was to communicate needs to the public through his weekly news conferences. Dreyfus worked to overcome the automatic Wisconsin suspicion of "government getting into anything to do with the family" that he said grew out of the state's strong Catholic and Lutheran traditions.

Summary

The Dreyfus governorship was based more on the personality of the man and less on the new or global policy initiatives he gave to Wisconsin. His emphasis on tax reform was extremely popular and both protected and curbed human services programs. Dreyfus's efforts to cut or limit taxes shielded the property tax from citizen-imposed limitations. His decision, however, to refund the general-fund surplus slowed the inflation-driven growth of health and welfare spending.

As governor, Dreyfus believed his communicator/statesman role was best for the state and best suited to his public-relations talents. "Me being a non-legislator . . . I thought it was the way in which I could contribute the most. For a minority governor, the real job is to get to the people, and they will get to the legislators and you'll get your agenda done." His method proved successful in his high-profile fight for tax reform.

Dreyfus mostly concentrated on identifying concepts and serving as chairman of the board. He left management and implementation to an active cabinet. He was not afraid to solicit ideas or ask questions.

He was criticized for allowing too many trial balloons to rise from administrative meetings. Many ideas were labeled ill-conceived, like the one offering a free medical-school education in exchange for five years of service in an isolated community. His office sometimes was described as a "side show" that offered little in terms of substantive change.

Dreyfus' disinterest in the final details of legislation contributed to the criticism that he performed little personal follow-through with the legislature.

"You could defeat him on bill after bill and he'd never join you in the debate," said state Representative John Norquist. "If you take policy really seriously, it's not much fun to have the main adversary walk away."

Dreyfus said he didn't view himself as "some kind of a super-legislator sitting in the governor's office." He said he had no real drive to get his own programs passed. "I clearly took the position, as I used to with my faculty, if they can find a better way to get where I want to go, that's fine with me," he said. "I couldn't give a damn whose name was on the bill or the jacket."

To the surprise of many, Dreyfus decided to be a one-term governor. He said he might have considered reelection had Wisconsin not changed from two-year to four-year gubernatorial terms, but he did not have an agenda to fill another four years.

"I might have accomplished more things in the first year of a new term, but then the remaining three years would be the same old Mickey Mouse of a minority governor dealing with this overwhelming majority on both sides," he said. "Essentially what I went down to Madison to do, I felt, was accomplished."

9

Massachusetts

MICHAEL DUKAKIS, DEMOCRAT, 1975-1979; 1983-1991

Context

The English Puritans who landed at Provincetown in 1620 ran Massachusetts without competition for more than two centuries. But the arrival of thousands of Irish Catholics fleeing a potato famine in the 1850s began a century of ethnic hostility as Irish and Italian immigrants fought with their Yankee predecessors for political power. Racial conflict is a relatively recent phenomenon in Massachusetts, where blacks constitute only 3.8 percent of the state's 5.7 million people. Tensions are concentrated in older cities, including Boston, where nearly one resident in four is black. School desegregation became a battleground in the late 1960s and early 1970s and focused attention in Boston on ethnic, class, and racial problems.

The politically active Irish helped make Massachusetts one of the most Democratic states in the country. It was the lone state to cast its electoral vote for George McGovern over Richard Nixon in 1968. Dwight D. Eisenhower and Ronald Reagan are the only Republican presidential candidates to carry Massachusetts since 1928, and both Reagan margins were narrow. Democrats in 1980 were split between Jimmy Carter and independent John Anderson.

Only two Republican members of Congress—Silvio Conte and Margaret Heckler—were elected between 1974 and 1990. Heckler, from the Boston suburbs, was defeated following redistricting in 1982.

Governor Michael Dukakis defeated the last Republican governor, Francis Sargent, in 1974. Another Democrat, Edward King, handed Dukakis a bitter primary defeat in 1978. After sitting out four years, Dukakis came back in 1982 to serve two more terms. During his third term, he became the Democratic presidential candidate against George Bush in 1988.

Dukakis presided over the highs and lows of the state's roller-coaster economy. The 1973 oil embargo, a national recession, and rampant inflation had brought Massachusetts to the brink of bankruptcy when Dukakis was first elected. The end of the space race slowed growth in science-based industries. By 1975, an unemployment rate of more than 12 percent was the second highest of any state in the country.

Recovery in the late 1970s was kindled by the state's 117 institutions of higher education, such as Harvard and the Massachusetts Institute of Technology. Computer, medical, and defense employers moved in as the schools produced high-tech spin-off firms and a steady supply of young business and engineering professionals.

With prosperity came pressure for more government spending. The state was dubbed "Taxachusetts" as taxes were raised to meet state and local government commitments to social and educational programs. Massachusetts, the fifth smallest state in the nation, was second only to Alaska, the largest state, in the amount of property tax collected. High-tech industry leaders were among those who rebelled by supporting Proposition 2 1/2, a successful 1980 referendum limiting property taxes to 2 1/2 percent of valuation. It was bitterly opposed by cities, which were dependent on the property tax as a main source of revenue, and labor unions, which correctly anticipated the loss of 40,000 public-sector jobs.

During the national recession of 1981-82, Massachusetts's unemployment rate rose to nearly 8 percent. But by 1985 it consistently reported the lowest unemployment of any of the nation's industrial states.

The mid-1980s saw Massachusetts riding the crest of high-tech growth, and state revenue collections soared. Because the governor has a lot of authority on budget matters, Dukakis was given credit for engineering a "Massachusetts miracle." Critics argued, however, that the economy would have improved no matter who was governor.

The economy showed signs of weakening again in 1988. The state faced severe fiscal problems as the decade ended. Foes blamed Dukakis for having spent too freely during the years of economic optimism. Dukakis loyalists were just as quick to blame the trouble on the Reagan cutback in federal assistance and passage of Proposition 2 1/2, which required dramatic increases in state aid to local government.

Profile

Michael Dukakis was born 3 November 1933, in the affluent suburb of Brookline, Massachusetts, which remains his home. After graduating from Swarthmore College in 1955, he served a two-year army hitch, mostly in South Korea. He earned his law degree from Harvard in 1960 and practiced law until 1974. He was elected to the state House of Representatives in 1963, ran unsuccessfully for attorney general in 1966, and lost a bid for lieutenant governor in 1970, after giving up a safe state House seat.

As moderator of public television's "The Advocates" from 1970 to 1973, Dukakis gained visibility and honed TV skills that helped him beat Republican incumbent Francis Sargent in 1974, becoming one of many Democrats who won governorships in the aftermath of Watergate.

Dukakis had campaigned on a reform platform, promising to eliminate patronage and improve fiscal management of state affairs, criminal justice, and mental health. Most of all, he had promised no new taxes. However, he inherited a $450 million deficit in the state budget, and before the year was out, he reluctantly approved a $362 million tax increase.

Although the economy was on the upswing, Dukakis accumulated foes during the term now called "Duke I." His so-called "meat-cleaver" approach to welfare reform, which cut 15,000 to 18,000 people from assistance, was described by one former supporter as a "war against the poor." Legislators were critical of Dukakis's aloofness and tendency to pontificate. Ethnic groups, particulary the Irish and Italians, considered him condescending and standoffish on patronage questions. Edward King, riding a wave of "anybody but Dukakis" sentiment, won the 1978 Democratic primary that ousted Dukakis after one term.

King, however, was perceived as the inept head of a scandal-ridden administration prone to padding expense accounts. He frequently was forced to defend controversial expenditures on first-class travel, dry cleaning, and lavish lunches of lobster salad sandwiches.

Dukakis, meanwhile, retooled his image and his issues at Harvard's Kennedy School of Government. He came back to beat King in a 1982 primary rematch, then easily won the general election over Republican John Sears. The Dukakis who returned to the governor's office in 1982 for eight more years ("Duke II") was more of a coalition builder. Biographers Charles Kenney and Robert Turner of the *Boston Globe* said Dukakis became "a sensitive listener." "Rather than apolitical and sanctimonious," they wrote, "he would become an inside player, a loyal political friend."[1]

Thankful for "something that one rarely gets in American politics—a second chance," Dukakis presided over a period of sustained political and economic success in Massachusetts. Backed by a strong economy, Dukakis took firm control of the state's Democratic Party and state government. He championed a major welfare reform program and pioneered statewide universal health-care insurance. Dukakis easily won reelection to a third term and soon afterward became the Democrats' 1988 presidential nominee.

After losing to George Bush, Dukakis returned to Boston to complete his third term. He announced early in 1989 that he would not seek reelection. His lame duck status diminished his clout and contributed to the turmoil in state finance. With high-tech production slowing and a once-booming housing market in the doldrums, Dukakis and the Democratic-controlled legislature entered 1990 with a $600 million deficit in a $12.8 billion state budget.

Education

K-12 education in Massachusetts is heavily dependent on the local property tax. School districts looked to the state to offset the impact of Proposition 2 1/2. Clearly, the voter-imposed ceiling on property taxes muted the general populace's call for educational reform, particularly reform that cost money.

Dukakis and the chairpersons of the legislature's education committees jointly introduced an educational finance bill in the fall of 1983, but it never got off the ground. It was a top-down approach to reform, with the state board of education mandating standards for teacher competency and student achievement. It ignored local control, tax constraints, and politics and carried a hefty price—$450 to $500 million.

Not until July 1985 was there a successful K-12 education reform bill. Dukakis, said education advisor Nancy Richardson, proposed a much leaner bill with the endorsement of the Massachusetts Teachers' Association. The new, pared-down package had a price tag of $80 million. It provided for less than the 10 percent pay hike teachers originally had requested. Still, the bill gave districts the option, with state assistance, of raising teachers' minimum base to $18,000. Before the bill, starting salaries ranged from $12,000 to $16,000 around the state.

The legislative committee heads "took very strong control the second time so that the bill would not get out of hand again," said Richardson. "They steered it through so it wouldn't involve too many programs and too much money."

The legislature acceded to the demands of local school boards and backed off state-mandated teacher and student standards. Instead, teachers were given incentive grants to help them take advantage of professional growth opportunities. Dukakis asked for and got more dollars for districts with low property tax bases and large numbers of educationally disadvantaged pupils. Dukakis, who had watched the legislature amend the bill he had introduced earlier in the session, said at the signing ceremony: "I'm signing a better bill than the one I filed." The governor could take credit for framing the bill's objectives and motivating his staff to work with the legislature and varied teachers' groups to achieve necessary consensus.

The required funding came out of general revenue without tax increases. With appropriations increasing each year, the package added more than $600 million in aid to education during the first four years it was in effect.

The Public School Improvement Act of 1985 and a companion measure passed in 1987 rested on a statehouse consensus that it was more useful to establish strong, clear, thoughtful incentives for improvement than to try to impose change through the education bureaucracy. It also rested on a more realistic understanding of the state's budget restraints.

"The history of education reform over the past ten years has shown that the top-down approach has not been the real answer," said Richardson. "Our bill was unique because it provided a lot of local control at the same time it provided funds for remedial help." The decision to target resources on poorer areas helped build support, as did a change in the state's legislative leadership.

Dukakis worked closely with the teachers' union and key lawmakers to find ways to improve the educational system. In the process, he moved Massachusetts toward equalizing educational opportunities and kept his 1982 campaign promise to work for higher teacher salaries.

Health

While the ideology of New Federalism emphasized health-care cost containment, Dukakis saw health care as the individual right of every resident and committed his administration to provide it. The governor said he had believed in a comprehensive health-care system since Harry Truman. "One way or another, we pay for the poor and uninsured," Dukakis indicated. "Insurance companies raise premiums and hospitals shift costs for uncompensated care."

With approximately 7 percent of the state's population not covered by health insurance, Dukakis supported passage of the Massachusetts Health Security Act and signed it into law on 21 April 1988.

Massachusetts already had an Uncompensated Care Pool funded by a surcharge on all insurance premiums. It provided free hospital care for the uninsured and retired bad hospital debts. But the pool, scheduled to expire in October 1987, was controversial on several fronts. It had grown in three years from $200 million to $300 million. The surcharge had reached 12.5 percent by fiscal year 1986-87 and showed no signs of abating. Payers were upset that 60 percent of the fund was spent on unpaid hospital bills rather than free care for the uninsured.

Dukakis seized the debate over the Uncompensated Care Pool as an opportunity to launch his universal health care initiative. He and the legislature appointed a commission to examine how to provide and pay for health care for all citizens, not just the medically indigent. But because Dukakis was heavily involved in the presidential campaign by then, he designated his chief of staff, Hale Champion, to take the lead on the initiative. With Dukakis keeping close tabs on progress, the commission made its recommendations to the legislature in September 1987.

The first bill proposed by the commission stalled in the House of Representatives. Opponents included the Massachusetts Hospital Association, which argued the bill offered too little reimbursement for services rendered and too many restrictions on collection of bad debts. Small businesses objected to the fiscal impact on them. The measure was returned to the House Ways and Means Committee for further work, despite the backing of the insurance industry, labor unions, and consumer groups.

Champion, with instructions from Dukakis, worked with the chairman of the Senate Ways and Means Committee to forge an effective executive-legislative link. They supervised the give-and-take with the primary interest groups until the legislation passed. The final bill reestablished the Uncompensated Care Pool and provided incentives for employers to provide health insurance for employees. Employers who didn't provide insurance plans were required to make nonreimbursed payments into the fund. Small businesses were allowed to phase into the program. Individuals not covered by employers could obtain health insurance through other programs at state-subsidized rates.

The bill put 50 million more dollars into hospital reimbursement as a way to win support of the hospitals, who claimed they were being hurt by Medicare and Medicaid cutbacks. It also capped the responsibility of the private payers' surcharge for maintaining the fund. Once the cap is reached, the state uses general fund revenue to help make up any shortfall.

Welfare

Dukakis returned to office in 1983 determined to change what he believed was a flawed effort by the previous administration to provide job opportunities for welfare recipients. Based on jobfare experiments initiated during his first term, he was convinced that a combination of job training, child care, and extended health benefits could help thousands of welfare families to achieve independence and self-sufficiency.

An interdepartmental directive from the governor ordered all state agencies to set a unified goal of getting welfare recipients into the work force. The culmination of their effort was the Employment and Training Choices program—"ET."

Dukakis got federal approval and $8 million to make ET a Work Incentive program (WIN) demonstration project. To encourage state employees out of their traditional roles as custodians of benefits, Dukakis awarded certificates of merit to staff members who met benchmark goals of helping welfare recipients become independent.

Dukakis didn't even announce ET until the pilot project was nine months old and 6,100 welfare recipients had been placed in jobs. He then announced it with a flourish. His goal was to put 50,000 welfare recipients to work in five years. No major new legislation was required, Dukakis said, but budget increases were needed for expanded services. He was able to secure legislative support for the extra funding.

"ET is proving that when welfare recipients are given a genuine opportunity to work, they'll pick work over welfare every time," Dukakis said.

The components of ET were: an employment network; on-the-job training with initial salary paid by ET; education and training, including preparation for the high-school equivalency degree; and career assessment and planning. Additional support elements were child care, transportation, welfare benefits, and Medicaid. All welfare recipients were required to register for ET, but they were permitted to choose the components of the program most appropriate to their need. If recipients chose to do nothing, said Public Welfare Commissioner Chuck Atkins, they could "stay at home and try to live on $6,400 a year."

By 1990, more than 70,000 welfare recipients were in full- or part-time jobs and 75 percent of them managed to get off welfare completely. The average cost per client for ET training and support was $5,700, while an average of $12,650 was saved in AFDC, Medicaid, and food stamps benefits. The average ET full-time job paid over $15,000, not including benefits, compared to a $7,250 maximum AFDC grant to a family of three. For every $1 invested in ET, Massachusetts said it gained $2 in reduced welfare benefits and increased income tax revenues.

Critics suggested that early evaluations neglected issues of skimming and did not separate out people who would have graduated from welfare without ET. Debate over the success of ET continued into the final year of Dukakis' term.

Dukakis' involvement in ET was described as "knee deep and hands-on." He brought the departments and agencies together in 1983 and declared: "This is my priority. Do it." He directed, empowered, and enforced. This coordination and facilitation was critical to ET's success.

During the presidential campaign, the *Des Moines Register* credited Dukakis with "converting the Massachusetts Welfare Department from an anti-cheating agency to a job-seeking unit with much closer ties to the private sector."[2] *Newsweek* said ET should be a national model because "every family off welfare is one less family the federal government has to support. This program should be part of a national deficit-reduction strategy."[3]

Even Dukakis critics like the *New Republic's* Robert Kuttner called ET "Dukakis at his best."[4]

Summary

Dukakis's popularity reached an all-time low as he prepared to leave office. Analysts debated how much credit or blame to give the governor for the peaks and valleys in the state's economy:

The State House has been abuzz the last six months with stories of Dukakis being disengaged from his job and lacking the political will and clout to be effective.

"He's become irrelevant," said (Richard) Manley of the (Massachusetts) Taxpayers Foundation. "The problem is that nobody likes a loser. The view of the people in Massachusetts is that they won't forgive him for losing. And they think he's lied about the precipitous drop in revenues. They think he was lying about the miracle and everything else."[5]

Dukakis never was far from remembering that, in his earlier "Duke I" incarnation, he was trounced by a fellow Democrat. Duke I earned Dukakis his reputation as an aloof, arrogant technocrat. Duke II ran for president.

"I'm a much better coalition builder these days than I used to be," he said at the height of his popularity. "One of the lessons I've learned, at times painfully, from Duke I is that you can be most successful in this business if you can bring people together."

Returning from the presidential campaign, Dukakis struggled to keep the pieces of state government held together. The state went deeper into debt as 1990 progressed, while Dukakis and the legislature failed to resolve budget issues.

Long-time Dukakis watcher Robert Turner of the *Boston Globe* said Dukakis had serious problems his third term because he failed to respond effectively to criticism.

"He has been the object of quite a tide of criticism, much of it really personal and abusive, and a lot of it factually pretty far off base, but he hasn't been able to counter it," said Turner. "He's been an easy target and he's not made it any harder on them. He's not fighting back."

The governor, however, correctly noted that several of his colleagues in bordering New England states were also in trouble. "The region's economy is down," he said. "Many governors are not running for reelection."

Dukakis' use of the Massachusetts miracle in the campaign for the presidency, he noted, made him "understandably vulnerable to attack" when the state's economic fortunes declined. "Had I not run for the presidency," he continued, "I might have been able to respond to the economic problems earlier. But the differences in my response likely would have been at the margin."

Charisma clearly was not Dukakis's long suit. But his basic decency and values were consistent with Massachusetts's liberal reputation. His willingness to spend more on increased government services was consistent with the state's economy during the boom years.

Dukakis, while learning to collaborate in order to build consensus, was directive when solutions were within his reach. He empowered and sustained those who carried out his directions. As a general manager, he set the goals, then got the right people to meet them.

Massachusetts, with Dukakis as governor, was on the cutting edge of change in education, health, and welfare. The long-term impact of his actions remains to be determined, however. Continuing budget deficits could impede future activism and mute Duke II initiatives. But as a Democratic governor in a heavily Democratic state, Dukakis had the power to shape events. He did so. After he lost the presidency in November 1988, Dukakis returned to Boston saying, "I still have the second best job in the world."

Notes

1. Charles Kenney and Robert L. Turner, *Dukakis: An American Odyssey* (Boston: Houghton Mifflin Company), 152.

2. David Westphal, "Ambitious Job Program Curbs Welfare Dependency," *Des Moines Register*, 24 May 1987, sec. A, p. 1.

3. Tom Morganthau, "Welfare: A New Drive To Clean Up the Mess," *Newsweek*, 2 February 1987, 24-25.

4. Robert Kuttner, writing in *The Boston Globe* (September 1985), quoted in Kenney and Turner, 191.

5. George E. Curry, "Dukakis Gets Flak for Failed Miracle," *Chicago Tribune*, 16 December 1989, sec. C, p. 1.

PART THREE

Lessons Learned:
Leadership and the Governors

10

Diverse Leadership Styles:
Diverse Results

The eight governors under our microscope are as varied generationally as they are geographically. Winter, the eldest, was born in 1923 as the nation enjoyed peace and prosperity. He was 56 when he took office in Mississippi in 1980 in a world that had been reshaped by the atom, the cold war, integration, and technology.

The youngest of the governors studied in this report, White of Texas and Janklow of South Dakota, were born in 1940 and 1939, as a nation still reeling from the Depression prepared for war. Like Lamm of Colorado, Janklow was 39 when he was inaugurated in 1979—the two youngest of the lot upon taking office.

Although their paths were different—the group includes poor boys and patricians, five lawyers, an educator, a banker and a businessman—each came to the governorship well-prepared. Dukakis of Massachusetts, Evans of Idaho, Lamm, Snelling of Vermont, and Winter had been legislators, while Janklow and White both claimed legal and electoral success as state attorneys general. Only Dreyfus came from "outside" the statehouse milieu, and he had been right around the corner in public education.

Tempered by the pragmatic demands of governing, all could be classed as moderates. The partisan labels that split them 5-3 between Democrats and Republicans disappeared quickly when they discussed their goals for their states and the strategies they had used to achieve them.

The case studies reveal substantial differences in the governors' style, political skills, and management ability. The governors also differed widely in their degree of planning, commitment, and willingness to delegate. None of the group approached all areas of concern with equal interest, commitment, and talent. Each had different priorities. Each could tally his own satisfactions and frustrations.

Responses to New Federalism

Although the states provided the laboratories, Ronald Reagan and the economy provided the catalyst. The states had shown they could instigate and innovate, but they often required a national nudge or a federal partner. New Federalism provided the needed push.

In dispersing responsibilities and costs, Reagan gave the states renewed clout in education, health, and welfare. Whether the president's goal was to realign the federal system or reduce the federal budget, the result was to grant new power to states that would claim it. Some took the challenge; others flinched.

All the studied governors, with the exceptions of White and Dukakis, were on the job when Reagan was elected. Dukakis had already sampled the frustrations of dealing with the federal government during his first outing as governor.

For some of the governors who presided over the transition to New Federalism, the Reagan initiative presented an opportunity to be more creative and flexible. It gave others a chance to fulfill campaign promises to roll back government. Still others saw New Federalism as a negative force that coerced innovation as a way to endure new budget cutbacks.

None of the governors in this study, even the most partisan, entirely resisted the notion of New Federalism. Most, however, warned their constituents that demands for increased state and local government services would bring a need for more state and local revenue. The governors believed Reagan had not really sorted out the division of roles and responsibilities between federal, state, and local governments. But if they could live with increased demands on their state budgets, all the governors saw advantages in the promised reduction of federal regulation.

South Dakota's Janklow, for instance, was chafing under what he saw as federal over-regulation. He had locked horns with Washington over issues ranging from the packaging of government handout cheese to the bounty system he had devised to encourage state employees to collect child support from negligent parents. "Of all the areas I dealt with as governor," Janklow said, "none was more frustrating than the regulatory climate in Washington."[1]

The new Reagan drive to reduce the federal government's role complemented Janklow's campaign promise to apply business disciplines to state government. In some areas, like the work incentive and community work experience programs, Janklow was one step ahead of New Federalism and found his efforts advanced and validated by the new federal philosophy. Ironically, Janklow got nowhere with his "Renaissance in Federalism." The state's offer to accept a cut in federal payments while taking over administration of all federal social-service programs was rejected.

Like Janklow, Dreyfus was ready for the Reagan initiatives. A 1979 Wisconsin study of welfare had found the rigidity of federal legislation to be a key problem. Eighteen months later, New Federalism gave the state what Dreyfus called "a very real opportunity to begin to do some of the things we wanted to," such as increasing child support enforcement and work incentives and establishing an educational training office.

Vermont's Snelling, the third Republican governor studied, was a skeptic on New Federalism. "I don't think there's been a New Federalism," he said. "There never was. There has been a reduction of federal funding but there's been no realignment whatsoever, really, in responsibility." In practice, several governors said, New Federalism was more a label under which the federal budget might be cut than a pervasive realignment of basic functions. Most also came to believe that many key regulatory controls were never really devolved: The states were still stuck with federal mandates, often without matching federal dollars.

Snelling, who was chairman of the National Governors' Association from 1982 to 1983, pushed hard for a "sorting out" of responsibilities. Congress should set the minimum living standards to be guaranteed to all Americans, he said, but the federal government should then get out of the way while state and local governments handled the actual delivery.

Some of Congress's rule making, Snelling said, "is moral paternalism, and some of it is power seeking . . . and some of it is also crap."

At first, Colorado's Lamm welcomed New Federalism's promise to "sort out" which level of government should take responsibility for which functions. But like Snelling, Lamm came to believe that the promise was never kept. "Overall, I think Ronald Reagan's New Federalism simply was an abandonment of a bunch of areas the federal government had been in. . . . I don't think his intention was to rethink the federal system in terms of allocation of power."

Lamm acknowledged there had been "some letup" in federal intrusiveness: By the time he left office the state had more ability to act independently. Still, the letup was "not as much as everybody would like, not as much as Reagan promised."

Massachusetts Governor Dukakis, who substituted the label "New Feudalism" for New Federalism, was the harshest critic of the Reagan policies. In contrast to Reagan, Dukakis said, Richard Nixon was a true new federalist. Nixon used block grants to give the states support and discretion while seeking better coordination, Dukakis said. "Nixon didn't just say, 'See you later. We're walking away from this. Good luck.'"

For most governors, New Federalism presented a good news / bad news dilemma: The loss of federal dollars was offset by the promise of less regulation and more flexibility. In this context, however, it was hard to see a silver lining in states with looming economic troubles. Clearly, distressed economies sharply limited the options available to governors who couldn't easily go to taxpayers or legislatures for new dollars to respond to federal policy shifts.

Mark White came to office in Texas assuming that a state budget surplus would let him keep his promise to raise teacher salaries. But just after his election he learned that, instead of a positive cash flow, the state would face a several billion dollar deficit. The discovery also chilled his determination to initiate new programs to help the medically indigent. Ultimately, however, White helped create a context in which changes could occur—changes that surprised observers who associated Texas only with tight budget policies, conservative biases, and Reaganomics.

Perhaps Winter in Mississippi and Evans in Idaho had the most trouble adjusting their budgets to the Reagan mandates. Both states already were playing catch-up in social spending when New Federalism hit. The new federal policies, however, were compatible with Winter's own view of reform as the consolidation of existing programs to achieve more efficiency and greater benefits. "The proliferation of governmental entities in order to perform additional services, it seems to me, has probably been carried to an extreme at both the federal and state level," he said.

New Federalism found Idaho's Evans already struggling to cope with a regional recession. As far as the governor was concerned, very little was left to cut. In most areas of education, Evans contended, Idaho was so far behind that catch-up funding was needed before reform could even start.

But as more Reagan Republicans were elected to the Idaho legislature, Evans recognized the new political realities and began to pare his already austere budget. With the resulting cost-cutting proposals, an *Idaho Statesman* editorialist wrote, Evans "seized the initiative in the setting of the state budget."[2] By thus taking the lead, the *Statesman's* "best goalie"[3] was able to retain threshold services and reduce the effect of the legislature's meat-ax approach.

Fiscal Consequences of New Federalism

The states that most aggressively picked up the federal slack were those with the longest progressive tradition, regardless of what party was on top. Massachusetts, Vermont, and Wisconsin—high-tax states all—each had given significant tax relief shortly before the Reagan policies took effect. Nevertheless, all three were able to buffer the impact of the cuts.

Massachusetts saw a remarkable period of change, featuring such programs as school finance reform, a new employment-and-training thrust for welfare, universal health insurance, and quadrupled scholarship aid. But Dukakis gave New Federalism no credit for inspiring state innovation. "It wasn't because somebody yanked something away that we went in," he said. "This was something we wanted to do and worked very hard to do." Although it was later to slow down, the rapidly expanding Massachusetts economy of the time appeared to permit expansion of state resources and facilitate Dukakis initiatives.

Even through the 1982 recession, Vermont kept its social programs going. Looking to the future, Snelling urged the state to break the habit of sopping up the surplus in good times and "slaying sacred oxen" to make ends meet in bad. While he was able to win legislative approval of a "full cycle" fiscal policy during his term, the concept was abandoned by his successor.

Wisconsin's ability to pick up the revenue-sharing slack in the midst of recession depended on a sales tax hike. Lee Dreyfus campaigned as energetically to raise taxes in 1982 as he had campaigned to lower them in 1978. At least one observer believed Dreyfus—by forestalling a Wisconsin version of the tax revolt that was sweeping the nation—had protected the balance between state and local government and preserved the level of state services.

The budget cuts and sluggish economy also let Dreyfus make institutional changes he couldn't have undertaken in a time of plenty. "That's when you learn to manage," he said. "You don't manage in a period of inflationary increases and new money." Dreyfus's economies included consolidating cabinet-level agencies and dropping a branch campus he saw as politically vulnerable and unnecessary.

Janklow in South Dakota agreed that hard times can give managers an advantage. He took advantage of the crunch to reallocate resources through deinstitutionalization, work incentives, and consolidation. "They don't argue with you when times are bad about taking some cuts," he said. "If you're flush you can't do it." Overall, Janklow generated selective cuts. But he managed to maintain the overall level of social services.

Lamm also saw a constant erosion of revenues and faced the corresponding need to slash state spending. Some marginal programs and inefficiencies were eliminated. But Lamm balked at giving New Federalism too much credit for inspiring economies: "That's more making a virtue of necessity," he said. "I don't think it was intended."

In Lamm's view, Colorado squeezed through the fiscal crisis by passing the buck, shifting costs to local government. The president's "anti-tax, anti-spend, cut-government tone" was contagious, he said. "Reagan's tone hit the state of Colorado and the state of Colorado said 'whoopie,' and we cut taxes, too." Instead of reducing spending, Lamm argued, the state should have stepped in to pick up the federal slack.

Mississippi, with the lowest per capita income of any state, had to scramble to respond to the Medicaid cutbacks, and the adjustment continued through the 1980s. Despite increased efficiency and reduced Aid to Families with Dependent Children rolls, Winter said the state had to increase its Medicaid outlays to make each year's budget come out even. State-run medically needy programs have since been instituted to fill the gap.

In Idaho, recession had hit in 1979. As New Federalism was forcing cutbacks in social program funding, the public assistance rolls were swelling. The funding famine provided an opening for Evans. After rallying support from all over Idaho, he finally convinced the usually hostile legislature to adopt a 2.5 percent increase in sales taxes over a three-year period. "We used the constituency out there who strongly supported education, medical care. . . . We awakened them." Despite the federal cutbacks, Evans won credit for maintaining key programs.

White responded to the fiscal impact of New Federalism in the midst of a severe economic downturn in Texas. To win the increased school spending he sought, he linked the proposed educational package to a boost in highway funding. He was even more constrained in health and welfare. He resisted major increases to pay for health changes, preferring to juggle funds among existing programs. He did not initiate major changes in welfare programs.

Responses to Political Forces

Several governors were even more constrained by their legislative and political environments than by reduced federal outlays or declining state revenues. State political conditions either limited or expanded the governors' opportunities to respond to the period of change. Many built strong alliances with the legislative leadership. Some chief executives were able to craft strategic responses; others were more reactive.

Needing legislative support was one thing; securing it was another. Democrats Dukakis, White, and Winter and Republicans Snelling and Janklow enjoyed the sometimes-uncertain pleasure of having legislative majorities of their own parties. Often the fact that both the governor and the statehouse majority were of the same party meant little. Governors, who tended to be less ideological or partisan than legislators, often found grassroots or coalition support necessary to win more than single-shot victories on limited issues.

Although he had alienated legislative Democrats in his first term, Dukakis was careful to build bridges during his second. Instead of lecturing Massachusetts lawmakers, he worked closely with party leaders to forge an education compromise that he acknowledged as an improvement over the bill he himself had first filed.

As Dukakis had seen in his first term, merely having a legislature of his own party was not a one-way ticket to success. As far as Republican Snelling was concerned, his "only enemies" were conservative Vermont Republicans who were resistant to change. After 14 years as majority leader, he said, "I would have been seriously disappointed if they hadn't attacked me." Snelling also used his troubles with GOP conservatives to win votes elsewhere. "Sometimes I would even needle somebody to guarantee that he would say something horrible about me or my program, which would almost assure that I'd be able to get Democratic support."

For Janklow, GOP party ties were strong and held tight, until his difficult last year. The Republicans, who had lost both the governorship and the legislature during the administration of Democratic governor Richard Kneip, regained control with Janklow's election. The new Republican majority in the part-time South Dakota legislature appeared relieved to find a forceful leader of its own party. Until 1986, when he violated GOP orthodoxy by challenging a sitting U.S. senator of his own party, Janklow got near-blind support on all but his most controversial proposals.

"The party felt they kind of owed me that," Janklow recalled. "Some respected legislators would get up in caucus and say, 'Look, he is our governor and he's on our side and, by God, when we were campaigning last time he's the only guy you could count on.'"

Although some observers use "bullying" and "hardball" to describe Janklow's dealings with the legislature, he is generally credited with working effectively with lawmakers, forming coalitions with key GOP leaders and conscientiously keeping legislators informed.

In Texas, White developed close working relationships with powerful fellow Democrats in the legislative leadership. White's successful initiatives in education and indigent health care came only after he learned to piggyback on the influence of Lieutenant Governor Bill Hobby, who presided over the state Senate, and Speaker of the House Gib Lewis. The White legislative record offers a useful study in brokered politics, featuring committees, task forces, and the solid front presented by the governor, the lieutenant governor, and the speaker.

If Snelling occasionally had to outwit his GOP colleagues, and Janklow and White cashed in on loyalty and lobbying, Winter turned to another tactic to get his way. When his fellow Democrats in the legislature failed to move ahead on his education reforms, Winter said: "We decided that we would go to work."

Winter raised $100,000 for television and radio advertising and scheduled citizen forums all over state. It was not the usual way a Mississippi governor lobbies the legislature, but Winter got his program through. In the course of the effort, Winter claimed, both he and the legislature gained a new sense of what they could accomplish. "I had finally developed an effective relationship with the legislature."

It's almost impossible to write a happy scenario for a governor facing a legislature controlled by the opposing party: Republican Dreyfus and Democrats Evans and Lamm wrestled with opposing majorities in their legislatures.

Because he'd wrested the GOP nomination away from the party regulars, Dreyfus had some success as a maverick who could turn for help to the voters themselves or to the Democrats who firmly controlled the statehouse. He worked hard at bipartisanship, often outlining his legislative goals and letting lawmakers handle the details. "You guys have been at this a lot longer than I have," he'd say. "You ought to be able to do something better than I've done." But Dreyfus's cooperation with the Democrats and his disinterest in who got credit for legislative accomplishments ultimately angered the Republican leaders who should have been his natural allies.

In hindsight, Dreyfus would have done it differently. "I would have gotten active in the party. I simply had my own agenda. I could have used the party."

When Democrat John Evans succeeded to Idaho's governorship in 1977, the former lieutenant governor had a reputation for amicable relations with the state's GOP-controlled assembly. But relations quickly soured. By 1984, Republicans could muster the two-thirds vote needed to override an Evans veto with no help from the Democrats. Evans's temper frayed as he dealt more aggressively and directly with lawmakers.

Although he realized raising taxes can mean political death, Evans decided he must "go to the mat with the legislature" to enjoy a productive governorship. For Evans, as for Winter and Dreyfus, the answer was to build grassroots coalitions to bring external pressure on the legislature. Ultimately he won the sales tax increase he sought for schools. "With the legislature controlled strongly by the other party," he said, "we had to go out and mobilize the people first."

For the last eight years of Lamm's stint as governor, Republicans controlled both chambers of the legislature. By 1984, Democrats couldn't even muster the votes to sustain a Lamm veto. Nor did Lamm ever find a way to accommodate himself to the legislature. He often viewed lawmakers as obstructionist and reactionary. They saw him as intemperate and aloof. Lamm acknowledged he could have worked more amicably with legislators, but speculated that an enduring rivalry between the legislative and executive branches, "something built into Colorado," may also have been at work.

One Colorado result of New Federalism was an unsuccessful legislative attempt to amend the state constitution to take away the governor's authority to control federal funds. The face on the dart board was Dick Lamm's, but with fewer restrictions on federal money, the real issue was the executive-legislative balance of power.

The Range of Gubernatorial Powers

Why were some of the governors able to sell their pet programs while others failed or got just a portion of what they wanted? Our sample is relatively evenly divided between governors with weak institutional powers and those who had extensive power over state budgets, appointments, and the legislative agenda. The so-called "strong governors"—Dreyfus, Dukakis, Evans, and Janklow—had no automatic assurance of success, however.

Dukakis parleyed his powers and his relationship with the legislature into a string of second-term accomplishments. It is arguable that the strong personal stamp Dreyfus and Janklow put on their administrations also resulted from their ability to act and budget independently. But Evans's strong-governor powers couldn't fix the economy or mollify hostile legislators.

Both Winter and White had severely limited institutional powers but were able to score dramatic education reforms. Winter's style was transformational as he helped Mississippi find new values and hope. White worked as a broker, trading on his relationship with the lieutenant governor and the speaker of the house. His appointments of Ross Perot and Helen Farabee also gave him critical leverage in the education and welfare areas.

"Weak" governors, Lamm and Snelling, worked hard to develop their managerial muscles, perhaps to compensate for their lack of more formal powers. It was difficult for them, however, to get out ahead of their legislatures and mold values and policies for sustained periods. Even with a legislature of his own party and significant formal powers, Snelling longed for a parliamentary government, in which the governor would be the party leader and lawmakers' electoral fates would be joined with his. "One of the things the party does before the elections in a parliamentary system," Snelling said, "is to decide what the agenda is. To be the leader of a party in that sense would be helpful."

Lamm was bedeviled by both weak powers and a cantankerous legislature of the opposing party. He was left to seek legislative accomplishment within the narrow realm of cost containment, one of the few places his interests and legislators' coincided.

Lamm had successfully used grassroots tactics to win the anti-Olympic initiative that carried him to the governorship. But as governor, he had less luck when he sought to bolster his powers by public persuasion. A crusade for a severance tax early in his governorship was defeated by heavy mining industry campaign advertising, although the legislature later passed much of the program. In later years, Lamm lost again when he asked voters to revoke a ban on publicly financed abortions for indigent women. In the bully pulpit, he was more educator than leader: Coloradans listened to what he had to say, but didn't necessarily go home and write their legislators.

Perceptions of the Governor as Leader and Manager

Should a governor be a transformational value-laden leader or a broker; should a governor break new ground or apply tested solutions? We expect our governors to be leaders—people who do the right thing—as well as managers—people who do things right. But it does not necessarily follow that those who know what to do also know how to do it. "We waste a tremendous amount of time, effort, money, energy and emotion in governments," Snelling said, "because people simply don't know how to accomplish the process of change." Similarly, author David Osborne laments that the political intellectuals who foster new ideas are often "too cerebral and technocratic to stir the political juices."[4]

Is it not possible for the roles to combine and shift? A snapshot of the eight governors reveals distinctive leadership characteristics: Janklow, the limited-issue ramrod; Winter, the value giver; Lamm, the cerebral educator; Dukakis, the technocrat; Evans, the broker; Snelling, the manager; White, the coalition builder; and Dreyfus, the cheerleader. But the next time the shutter clicks, the images may change, at least temporarily. Dukakis and White step into the role of transformational leader, and Dreyfus dons the technocrat's garb.

Each governor had access to a sophisticated wardrobe of management styles. One issue might demand strong personal involvement, but success in another area might depend on delegation to strong appointees.

Of the governors studied, Dreyfus was perhaps the most consistent delegator. Having decided his job was to deal with external constituencies, he appointed trusted cabinet officials and delegated to them the nuts and bolts of running government. Although critics accused Dreyfus of having no interest in the daily grind of governing, the governor insisted on reserving the final vote for himself: "Once a decision was made, once I made it," he said, "then everybody goes with it."

At the other extreme, Janklow didn't need the final vote—he'd had the first. And if his orders weren't met, he didn't hesitate to force compliance. He was both delegator and delegatee. When the state colleges, for instance, refused to reconcile their incompatible accounting systems, Janklow threatened to withhold their budget requests from the legislature and got his way within a week.

Was that coercion? Janklow would say yes. "But most of what I did *was* coercion. John Dillinger once said you can do a lot more with a gun and a smile than just a smile."

Former management consultant Snelling delegated with characteristic consistency and discipline. "Delegation is no excuse for mismanagement," he said, and monitored his appointees closely. "It is imperative that you hire people in every area who know more than you do and who are better than you are."

Dukakis, too, knew how to delegate and, perhaps more importantly, knew how to extend his own reach through those he deputized. His delegation was not hands-off. He launched his education-and-training initiative with the simple statement to his cabinet secretaries: "This is my priority. Do it." So effectively had he empowered his agents that his welfare commissioner was said to need only to point in the direction of the governor's office to motivate and prod his staff to carry on.

Another effective delegator was Winter, who turned to a hard-nosed private sector manager to straighten out his Department of Public Welfare. He relied on another cabinet officer, the director of the state health department, to take the lead in the fight against infant mortality.

Mark White scored the delegation coup, however, by going outside government to name Perot to head Texas's Select Committee on Public Education. And White went on to empower Perot, first by delivering on his promise to give Perot free rein. Then, in his self-appointed role as committee member, White helped assure that the group ultimately would achieve consensus. Another strong White appointment was Farabee to head the Task Force on the Medically Indigent. The wife of a leading state senator, she was an acknowledged civic leader in her own right.

Selling the Program

The governor who seeks to be a change agent can work quietly through coalition building or dramatically through the thunder of the bully pulpit. All governors, to win election, have perfected their own techniques for getting their way. If he wanted to get his program past balky legislators, John Evans knew he would have more luck changing the political environment than changing their minds. "They were very set in their ways," he said. "So we needed to get the pressure from down home."

The cases in which governors have accomplished change without a firm base of support were rare: Lamm's drive to contain health costs was one example, Janklow's detours around federal regulators another. Only in Massachusetts—where the governor, key legislators, and the teachers' union pushed through the school package—did K-12 reforms pass without significant, governor-initiated pressure from broad-based grassroots constituencies.

In every other state studied, governors found they needed the help of citizen coalitions to push for education reforms:

- Mississippi's Winter worked with educators, private citizens, and business leaders to draw up plans for a series of statewide forums the governor hoped would become "the largest mass movement in the history of Mississippi." Forty-two forums were held, providing the nucleus of the 25,000 citizens Winter eventually called upon to help in the final lobbying push with the legislature.

- In Texas, parent groups and business and media leaders joined Perot to add heft to the White-Hobby-Lewis troika's push for an education package. Teacher groups eventually split over the teacher-testing proposal, although the package, in part, had grown from White's ties to teacher organizations. White, who had been thwarted in his first efforts to launch his education reforms, initially resisted the appointment of the select committee Perot was to head. But he ultimately came to see the committee as a means to create momentum for change—to, in effect, "light a fire" under the legislature.

- Janklow worked with affected school districts and business and civic groups to pass education initiatives such as a career ladder for teachers. Like White, Janklow sought—and sometimes got—the support of teacher organizations with whom he previously had developed a rapport. On school consolidation, the governor said, he got the South Dakota Education Association endorsement only after a "knock-down, drag-out fight."

- In Idaho, John Evans worked through teachers, parents, and business groups to win more money for schools while the governor's State Conference on Children pressed for improved programs in education and children's health and welfare.

The two governors who were frustrated in efforts to change their school systems—Snelling and Lamm—were unable to assemble effective support coalitions. Snelling's farsighted plan to change the state's school finance system was killed by school district and local government opponents who saw a threat to their tax revenues. Lamm blamed Colorado's "almost monomaniacal" belief in local control for the disinterest that greeted the recommendations of his bipartisan task force on school quality and equality.

As Dreyfus assessed Wisconsin's needs, "education was not on the front burner for reform in 1978." Dreyfus believed education policy should be made at the local level, although he unsuccessfully pushed teachers for a statewide competency testing plan. He said a major contribution he made to education was making school boards more accountable to taxpayers by showing on tax bills how many dollars went to education. Dreyfus was also proud to leave a "legacy of shifting" the responsibility for funding schools. His drive to increase the sales tax, he said, helped education by taking pressure off the property tax.

The reformers often rallied under the banners of economic development and local pride. White, for instance, capitalized on Texas's economic downturn to present educational enhancement as a key economic development investment for the state. Evans took advantage of a general perception that Idaho schools were not of high quality: "Idaho was the Mississippi of the West," he said. "Business leaders said if you can't provide basics for children, you're not going to be able to attract business and industry to the state." In Mississippi, too, Winter used state pride to galvanize support for his program. "The argument I used was that it was time we got out of last place: 'You know those other states are not going to be standing still, and we are last now. We are going to be so far behind we'll never catch up unless we start moving.'"

Clearly, the laggard economy made most governors of the early 1980s cautious about pushing for increased spending. Education seemed a natural because it could be tied politically to economic development. Education expenditures also rubbed elbows with the middle class; educational options benefited all income groups and were politically popular. Most governors believed no real political constituency existed to support health and welfare initiatives for the poor. Political leaders had to have an ideological or value-laden commitment to reform before they sought to improve human-services programs—particularly if they wanted to increase services. Even the most popular health and welfare initiatives ran a distant second to education in popularity. Governors who wanted to make a difference in social programs found coalition building essential:

- Massachusetts' universal medical insurance plan was very much such an exercise. The effort started with the establishment of a task force to reconcile the competing interests of hospitals, the business community, the insurance community, labor unions, and ordinary citizens. Ultimately, in mid-presidential campaign, Dukakis enlisted former Kennedy School colleague Hale Champion to help forge the final link between the interest groups.

- For each Evans initiative in the health and welfare area, the governor put together a separate constituency. He worked with religious leaders to orchestrate support for deinstitutionalization. Not-in-my-back-yard pressures ultimately gave way to what Evans describes as a community consensus that disadvantaged people deserve "the comfort of a neighborhood setting." By the time it was over, even the Governor's Mansion had a halfway house as a neighbor. To lobby his state emergency medical services plan through the Idaho legislature, the governor assembled support from the commissioners of all 44 Idaho counties. He worked with the elderly through Operation Independence to halt the trend toward institutionalization.

- In Wisconsin, Dreyfus relied on local coalitions of elderly citizens and advocacy groups to win approval for a Community Options program that initially had been resisted by nursing homes, health care providers, and counties fearful of hidden costs.

- In South Dakota, Janklow turned to the Association for Retarded Citizens to spearhead his deinstitutionalization drive.

Many gubernatorial failures to pass health and welfare initiatives were, in fact, failures in coalition building. Janklow's biggest disappointment, for instance, was his failure to win adoption for his Indian Health Care Improvement proposal. A central flaw in the campaign was that local interests didn't have an early sense of ownership in the program. The proposal was developed primarily in house, then tendered for support to the tribes, many of whom were deeply skeptical of Janklow because of his law-and-order stance against the American Indian Movement.

Snelling, who also got mixed marks as a coalition builder, was battered during two of his most ambitious quests for reform—school finance and the "maxicap" campaign to cap medical costs—precisely because he failed to form crucial coalitions and bring important stakeholders into the proposal. Snelling later reflected on the need to line up allies before launching an initiative: "Before you come to the conclusion that somebody's going to oppose an idea, ask yourself, who's going to have an interest in it? Who may be concerned about it? Who may need to know about it?"

In the Vermont Futures program, Snelling showed how adept he could be at building support. When the economic orthodoxy of the job-stimulation initiative was questioned, Snelling said, "legislators had to be told to do it." To deliver the message, the governor put together a broad-based lobby of citizens anxious for something to be done to address Vermont's troubled economy.

Even the most adroit coalition builder can hit a day when none of the usual public-policy brokers wants to deal, a day when it's time to go beyond the legislatures and special interests to rally the grassroots. For all the governors, then, the next step was to appeal to the general public through the media.

Most, however, viewed the media with mixed emotions. Dreyfus expressed the general gubernatorial perception that most reporters were "closet sports writers." "They really see it as wins and losses, and how many yards made down the field, and how many scores you made," he said.

Nevertheless, all the governors courted coverage, whether on a sustained or strategic basis. They knew they were good copy and generally knew how to become the center of a news story. They were aware of how important the media could be in framing public dialogue and debate. Even with his citizen coalition in place, Winter found it necessary to pull out the media stops to assure passage of his education program. Before he was done, Winter had used virtually every tool of public opinion available, ranging from paid television and radio advertising to massive phone banks, to rally grassroots pressure on the legislature.

Dreyfus used radio to create almost a town-meeting strategy. "My real strength," the governor said, "was communication: use a phone-in, talk to voters."

A favorite Dreyfus tool was the telephone talk show on a small-town station, a tactic that resonated through the community for days as citizens prepared to make their calls and then talked about them afterwards. Word of the governor's appearance would spread still further through the local press, which used such stories heavily and, Dreyfus said, gave the participants a lot of credibility. "In our state they read the daily," he said. "They memorize the weekly."

In a larger-than-life version of the phone-in strategy, Dreyfus asked his cabinet to help him field calls on a live, statewide television talk show designed to take his sales tax case to the people. Dreyfus also broke new ground when he opened his bullpen-style office to statehouse reporters, essentially making them part and parcel of governance.

Janklow, too, was quick to take to the bully pulpit to marshal public opinion, using his formidable persuasive and public speaking abilities to make his case. Here the symbolic power of the governor's office— whether called the imprimatur, the cachet of power, or, as Janklow described it, the "reservoir of trust"—was in full force. Besides, said Janklow, "everyone knew I was a little crazy, so that there was a certain amount of trust in everything that I did."

Lamm, too, won popularity with constituents for his outspokenness. Many voters disagreed deeply with some of his positions, but they always knew where Lamm stood. His ideas got broad media exposure. He was a master of the catchy phrases and compelling images that courted headlines as surely as they courted controversy. "I saw the press as my way of getting my issues out," Lamm said, "far more than my political party."

There is little evidence, however, that the bully pulpit can succeed in isolation. Even the most impassioned oratory may not be enough if the governor is not by instinct a coalition builder and does not enjoy the give-and-take of political compromise.

Notes

1. The governors' comments in this and the following chapter come from their colloquium discussions, 24-25 February 1988, and from interviews with members of the project staff conducted between February 1988 and June 1990.

2. "Evans Was Conservative," *Idaho Statesman*, 6 January 1981, sec. A, p. 8.

3. "John Evans Made the Best of Tough Times," *Idaho Statesman*, 4 January 1987, sec. F, p. 2.

4. David Osborne, *Laboratories of Democracy* (Boston: Harvard Business School Press, 1988), 332.

11

The Governors and the New Federalism: The Past as Prologue

To many, the 1980s brought a new vitality to state government. Governors, not mayors, were making the front pages of national journals and newspapers. Their response to the changes stimulated by the president's efforts to cut back federal responsibilities for social services and community development won the frequent attention, if not always the applause, of scholars, the business community, and community leaders. We were told that a new era had arrived or that an old era had returned. States once again were the laboratory for testing the relevance of policies and programs that respond to the poor, to urban problems, and to the needs of rural areas. Successful initiatives, if not replicated by Washington as part of a national policy, could and would be exported from state to state. Marble-cake federalism would fade away and a new, albeit undefined, partnership between state and federal governments would emerge. It would result in clear lines of responsibility for social policies and programs. It would shift and sort programs in an efficient and equitable manner.

Several explanations were offered for the more aggressive policy-making role of governors during the Reagan years or the era of the New Federalism. Some appear useful; others offer little explanatory value. For example, *Baker vs. Carr*, the Supreme Court's one-person-one-vote mandate, likely increased suburban, not urban representation in state legislatures. Although a higher educational level and *Baker vs. Carr* may have changed the character of legislatures, the assumption that legislators allowed governors a more active role on health, education, and welfare issues appears flawed. State legislatures remain dominated by conservative interests, by whites, by middle-class Americans, by individuals who by and large applauded the Reagan Revolution's overarching theme of limited government.

113

Similarly, while many of the current breed of governors were old enough to observe or to have participated in the many social changes that occurred during the 1960s, the link between their role in the 1960s and their role as governors is not always apparent. Sixties activism is not a one-to-one predictor of behavior in the governor's office of the 1980s. For the most part, the resumes of the 1980s governors reflected experiences similar to those of the governors of the 1950s and 1960s. Most came up the political route. A good number got their feet wet in legislative or other political offices. A small number came out of the business world; an even smaller number came from academia. Vietnam, Watergate, and the civil rights movement, perhaps made many governors more reflective about the fallibility and strengths of government. But it would be stretching our analytical skills and our acceptance of psychodrama to suggest a direct line between these three cataclysmic events and a governor's leadership style or agenda between 1980 and the present.

Certainly the economics of the 1980s in many states fostered a more activist breed of governor. Yet the response pattern among governors was dissimilar. In some states, a down economy stimulated governors to respond with maintenance-of-effort or cutback management; in other states, economic doldrums fostered efforts to push new policies, particularly policies that could be sold as relevant to economic development. States with booming economies and resultant surpluses found it relatively easy to move new policies and programs. But not all of them did so. Some governors used the moment to give back money to taxpayers or, as taxpayer surrogates, to local jurisdictions.

Ronald Reagan usually takes center stage in hypotheses accounting for the perceived increase in the role of governors during the New Federalism era. The president's rhetoric concerning sorting out responsibilities and shifting roles ostensibly prompted governors to think about new and innovative state initiatives. However, while the administration's short-lived "shift and share" construct concerning federal and state roles provoked debate at National Governors' Association conferences and the like, it remained for the most part on the drawing board. More important in gaining the governors' full attention was the cutback in federal assistance and the related movement toward block grants. All governors had to respond to the changing nature of the federal inventory. Some did so by cutting back on out-of-favor programs; some by substituting state for federal funds. Many tried to make up for diminished federal resources by better management; some shifted burdens to local governments. Constituencies and commitments built up through years of federal largess kept states focused on federal initiatives in social policy and in protecting favored programs. The governor's attention in many states was also secured by fear of losing power to the legislature. Put another way, the flexibility that traveled with the block grants granted the allocator significant new powers and responsibilities—a fact of life not lost on most governors and legislative leaders. Governor vs. legislature battles over who controlled the new federal money—or the old federal money now in a new bottle—led in many states to direct governor involvement in developing and initiating policy.

The fact that Washington appeared to some to abdicate responsibility for setting social priorities caused some observers to suggest that what seemed to be new state activism was merely a reflection of minimal federal activity. Put simply, the absence of something to write about out of Washington created a void and generated good copy, or at least copy, about the governors. Advocates of this viewpoint would argue that the purported increased activism of governors during the 1980s was mainly smoke and mirrors: These governors were no different from their predecessors. However, the fact that states were able to gain the extended attention of media and scholars alike suggests that state activity was something more than a mirage.

Perhaps all we can say about why governors appeared to play a more vital role in the 1980s than they did previously is that a unique constellation of events—an uneven economy, post Vietnam/Watergate reflections, federal budget cutbacks, fewer restrictions on federal aid, and a beginning dialogue concerning state roles fostered by the president— created the context within which states assumed social policy leadership. These exogenous events affected different states in different ways. Clearly, the local economic, political, institutional, and social milieu moderated the impact of national variables on the states and their governors. Just as clearly, the personality, experience, commitments, and competence of the respective governors helped shape their involvement in determining specific state agendas.

Several summary judgments resulting from the colloquium with the governors and the case studies are presented at this juncture. They offer insight into the role of governors in responding to an era of rapid change in federal social welfare policy. They suggest hypotheses for future study about the relationships between the leadership style or approach of the governor; the state's political, economic, and social environment; the formal and informal rules and behavior patterns governing state government; and the record of the governor or state concerning health, education, and welfare initiatives. Given the time and budget constraints associated with this effort, they provide a beginning for what we hope will be a continuing study of governors. In this context, each governor and each scholar/practitioner participating in this initial study agrees that states have for far too long been the orphans of the federal system. In part because of necessity (the federal budget deficit) and in part because of choice (the aggressiveness of many states) states likely will play an increasing part in defining and carrying out social policies, an activity once thought to be the exclusive province of the federal government.

Reform vs. Change

Most of the governors attending the colloquium and participating in the case studies had trouble defining the word "reform." To some, the term connoted a positive value judgment about what they did or did not do; a judgment premised more on hopes than actual results. "It was too early to define whether what we did was good or bad . . . we cannot at this juncture judge effectiveness," one governor said. "The term reform suggests final data concerning impact." Some of the governors said that to call their actions in response to the New Federalism reform indicates "far more rational premeditation" than they engaged in. "Most of our actions were not premised on carefully thought-out problem analysis or objectives . . . or on a plan . . . or a well defined strategy," said one. "We often had a partial or limited view of our states and of the things we needed to do. We knew something about the delivery systems in health, education and welfare—but rarely enough. Sometimes we acted or reacted based on intuition—windows of opportunity. We were not always basing our initiatives on a criticism of the past or what existed regarding services."

Use of the term reform was deemed inappropriate by the governors when the action taken was principally a reconfiguration or amendment of actual services. Similarly, reform did not seem to fit actions taken to maintain existing programs or to improve coordination and management. Yet the governors agreed that these actions seemed significant at the time. Reform, to the governors' regret, suggested concern "only about the services themselves," one participant noted. "Rarely is the word defined in terms of administrative processes."

According to the governors, the language of reform is long on ideological content and short on substance. To liberals, reform suggests more money and more equity in service delivery; to conservatives, it means more efficient service delivery and, often, fewer services. Reform language, according to the governors, serves better in a campaign than to describe or evaluate actions in office. Most would prefer words like change or response. Both are value neutral, they said. "Both allow us to add up what occurred . . . and define ways to measure benefits and costs."

Context for Change and Response

Clearly, each state's political and economic environment affected the number and kinds of initiatives available to the governors. A down economy, such as many of the states faced, limited the change or response options. "We could not go to the taxpayers or legislatures for new dollars or new programs in response to federal policy shifts" was a common comment from participating governors in the Midwest, West, and South. "We were lucky if we could maintain what existed that we wanted to maintain." Conversely, the booming Massachusetts economy of the early 1980s permitted the governor to seek major, sometimes expensive changes in state health, education, and welfare systems.

A sluggish economy allowed governors to cut back on programs they did not like or felt were not effective: "It gave us a card to play in reallocating funds and eliminating some programs." Interestingly, a sluggish economy also allowed governors to secure visible educational initiatives if they wanted to. While education was often a "big buck" item, the need to enhance the state's economic competitiveness enabled governors to enlist the help of difficult legislators and taxpayers' groups. Repeatedly, governors asked their constituents how their states could compete in the world if their schools were second class.

In addition to the economy, other local political and social variables also helped shape governors' ability to do or avoid doing things. Importantly, most governors felt that no real political constituency existed to support comprehensive health and welfare initiatives for the poor. They could go for educational improvements, some of which reflected major budget expenditures, because, as noted earlier, these programs could be sold as essential to the growth of the state. Educational improvements also rubbed elbows with the middle class; that is, educational options benefited all income groups and were politically popular. Constituencies that supported increases in social service budgets were not particularly strong in most states. Where they existed, they often focused on limited programs where the general public was convinced fairness required action, such as programs involving children.

Governors appear to have lent as much strength as they took from their political and institutional environments. For example, the fact that the governor of Texas was sensitive to the needs of the poor gave certain policies a fighting chance: "He may not have gone out in front, but by just being there, he made a difference," one activist said. "If we had his predecessor in office, we could not have made a dent. We were always operating on the political and budget margin." Similarly, the governor of Idaho helped create a context within which maintenance of social programs was possible. "He was a decent guy," a former colleague said.

"His convictions were known. He made it tough for the legislature to run over key social programs. He was a good gatekeeper if not always an effective advocate."

Some other interesting environmental observations: The cultural impact of Idaho's large Mormon population affected how the governor could respond to federal human-service changes and achieve his own objectives. The governor of Idaho tied his initiatives to the Mormon respect for the family. Anglo/Indian tensions and distrust helped foster an environment that ultimately made it difficult for the governor of South Dakota to secure a major Indian health-care initiative. The credence granted the business community in Texas made the governor's selection of a prominent corporate leader to head the educational reform study a stroke of genius. It fit the culture and assured an audience and some results. Massachusetts's history of liberalism granted the governor a head start in pushing significant changes in health insurance coverage, welfare policies and other areas. Vermont's and Wisconsin's traditional support for relatively high welfare benefits made it difficult for them to opt for across-the-board program reductions. Mississippi's troubled racial past necessitated sensitivity and required the new language of economic development to sell educational changes. The weak-governor system in Colorado and the legislature's reputation for fiscal penuriousness confirmed the Colorado governor's own ideological preferences. No major increases for social welfare spending were proposed.

Leadership Approaches, Change, and Response

All the governors participating in the colloquium and case studies showed an ability to lead their states, if by lead we mean the capacity to initiate or respond to policy, management, or program options to secure change or protect or maintain valued services. In doing so, they evidenced skills and leadership styles ranging from the normative to the managerial; from the power broker to the cheerleader/public communicator; from governance by fiat to governance by delegation and consensus building.

Certain governors appeared to reflect certain biases or tilts with respect to leadership style, biases or tilts that seemed to shape the results in their states. The governors of Mississippi, Massachusetts, and to some extent, Texas were the most prone to articulate and convey values to provide the frame within which policy initiatives would be debated by legislature and voters. Each was able to secure major, comprehensive system changes in at least one of the studied areas: health, education, and welfare. The governors of Colorado and Vermont illustrated a bias toward a managerial approach. They did not come to office with strong normative concerns about social services nor did they assume such a posture once in office.   Their focus was on trying to achieve better management, to improve coordination, and to find better people to staff agencies.   Their primary achievements, as articulated by themselves and local observers, were in cost containment, more efficient delivery of services, and better integration of services.   The governors of South Dakota, Idaho, and Wisconsin reflected styles or approaches to the governor's office that often generated limited policy, management, or program changes.   For example, the governor of South Dakota was a consummate one-person show. He had strong opinions and a strong personality.   He knew how to use power and to use it effectively.   He was not a planner nor did he encourage planning studies and the like.   His record is one of selective but not systemic change.   The governor of Wisconsin did not view himself, nor did he function, as a policy or value giver.   He was a messenger to the public, and a communicator of public sentiment.   Policy initiatives defined by staff were accepted by the governor if he felt they reflected the public's interest or wishes.   In this context, apparent citizen concern for high tax burdens and government accountability led the governor to focus on lowering and shifting tax burdens.   Idaho's difficult economy left the governor little room.   He nevertheless was able to use his considerable coalition-building and outreach skills to maintain key social services in the face of Reagan administration cutbacks.

Leadership and Structure

Almost half of the governors studied came from strong-governor states; that is, their offices provided them strong appointment and budgetary powers.   Interestingly, however, structure did not appear to be a major factor in determining a governor's ability to achieve major changes.   Put another way, a governor's ability to build coalitions in the legislature or among the populace often overcame structural deficiencies.   The lack of formal powers often cost governors time and required extraordinary efforts to move the legislature or the bureaucracy.   But action could be and was accomplished.

Leadership and the Legislature

Many of the governors found themselves forced or required to build alliances with the legislative leadership.   Texas would not have achieved educational or health changes without the visible support of the speaker of the house, the lieutenant governor (who was also president of the Senate), and the governor.   Observers said these three were essential to the passage of any major, new policies. Their support did not always guarantee passage, but its absence generally guaranteed defeat. Massachusetts could not have moved forward on health, education, and welfare initiatives had the governor not been willing to compromise with legislative and other leaders.

Even governors who enjoyed legislative majorities of their own parties were not assured automatic support. Governors generally tended to be less ideological or partisan than legislators from their own parties. Sometimes, they came from a different generation or constituency within the party; sometimes they won the right to campaign for governor against the wishes of party stalwarts. Once they gained access to the governorship, their perspective understandably was broader than many legislators', including many in the legislative leadership. Appeals to the public or key groups within the public and a willingness to negotiate—"to accept less than what we wanted"—were essential to governors anxious for more than single-shot victories on limited issues.

Leadership and Equity

Most of the governors were education governors. Their sluggish economies combined with the national concern for education evidenced in *A Nation at Risk* to give them an opening. A national and state environment had been created that granted educational proposals a reasonable shot at making it. Education initiatives were seen as affecting everybody—my kid and your kid. Education was not a poverty program. It was the favored issue focus of the majority of governors.

Health and welfare provided different problems and, to most governors, fewer opportunities. Except in Massachusetts and to some extent Texas, where the political environment and the governors' commitment facilitated major health initiatives, governors were careful in approaching each area. Clearly, the politically fragile coalitions supporting health and welfare initiatives—groups often advocating the interests primarily of the poor—caused most governors to go slow, to pick and choose rather than attempt comprehensive change.

Unlike education, where there were usually relatively few interested outside and inside groups to deal with, health and welfare seemed populated by a large number of disparate bureaucracies—public, nonprofit, and private. To most governors, it was a morass. It took more time than they could afford to identify the crucial players and their behavior patterns. More relevant, there were serious limits on governors' own powers to deal with providers of varied services, their related federal friends, and other supporters. While joining welfare to work or job training seemed popular, it was not generally linked, as it was in Massachusetts, to more comprehensive changes in the delivery system. Improved efficiency and maintenance of effort seemed the prevailing themes of the governors' involvement. It was common in the studied states for governors to delegate to key staff and to avoid hands-on leadership and management roles.

Leadership and the Media

Most of the governors had a love/hate view of the media. Individual reporters or commentators were seen as frustrated sports writers. As the governors saw it, reporters wanted winners and losers. They were seen as great at covering conflict but as lacking the patience and interest in getting out the facts that would help the public understand the issues.

Despite their suspicion, all of the governors sought media support. They were the stars and most of them knew how to get in the newspaper. The governors of Mississippi, Texas, and Massachusetts assiduously courted the media in moving their major initiatives. The governor of South Dakota was always making news and loved it. It fit his style and proved useful in efforts to work with and sometimes bludgeon the legislature. The governor of Idaho found the media helpful in getting out the message concerning the need for a tax increase and the need to "save" specific programs. The governor of Vermont, while wary of the media, developed ground rules in his relationship to the press and TV that permitted him to avoid having the media become the messenger. The governor of Wisconsin broke new ground in dealing with the media. In effect, he made them part of his office on a continuous basis. He ran an open office, bull pen style. The press and TV had access all the time. With sometimes unpredictable results, they became part and parcel of governance.

Leadership, Planning, and Evaluation

None of the governors considered themselves to be real planners and none were terribly concerned with evaluation of their deeds while in office. There were some real conceptual and practical differences among them, however, particularly concerning planning. For example, the governor of Vermont was more prone than most governors to foster strategic planning efforts prior to generating new initiatives. Conversely, the governor of South Dakota, like many of his peers, found the time spent on planning generally out of sync with the benefits. The governor of Vermont believed that staff planning (problem definition, development of objectives, definition of strategies for intervention) was crucial to long-term impact; the governor of South Dakota believed such efforts generally would not produce results much different than his own intuition or sense of what was possible.

Time, resource, and political constraints made comprehensive planning a luxury for all governors. Generally, the governors neither sought nor were presented with "opportunity costing" or risk analyses concerning policy, management, or program options on their table. Their gut instincts and the judgments of their immediate staff or cabinet contributed to go/no go decisions. Often decisions were made incrementally or as part and parcel of muddling through.

Evaluation of initiatives was generally a casualty of busy schedules and staff limitations. It was also a casualty of the negative perception of the value of extended analysis. "Evaluation required more time than we or our staffs could give," one governor said. "Evaluations tended not to give us specifics or to be linked to action. To have an effective evaluation system, you needed specific policy or program goals and measurements. We rarely had either. Evaluation may produce in the long run. But we had to act in the short run."

Not too surprisingly in light of the confusion in the evaluation literature, governors and their staffs, generally found it difficult to separate out the relationship between human services problems, causes, and proposals. Most could not explicitly trace the link between health care and health conditions; learning and education services; dependency, poverty, and diverse poverty policies. Failure to understand the tie between objectives and proposals, as well as between problems and what causes them, made development of explicit evaluation measures and cost-benefit analyses difficult, even if time permitted and the governor was supportive. Most of the governors and their staff seemed to use input rather than output criteria—dollars allocated to services provided rather than social indicators of quality-of-life changes—in evaluating policies or programs. Anecdotes of success were often the most practical products of evaluation. The results of studies, when favorable, were used in the fight to secure or maintain policies and programs.

Leadership and Obstacles to Change

The governors revealed relatively similar views of specific federal obstacles to change in their states. The unpredictability of federal rule making and budgets often caused frustration and limited their freedom to act. Block grants were a step forward, but they did not go far enough. Furthermore, the governors objected to rigid federal guidelines governing social policies and programs that might fit one state but not another. Only a few governors were able or willing to do what Governor Janklow did with seeming impunity: disregard the regulations and assume a "Bronx Defense."

Most of the governors found entrenched human-service bureaucracies and their related client groups difficult to move. Almost without exception, governors said they had found the public agencies administering programs to be adept at organizing beneficiaries and their advocates. When the governors wanted to change things that affected bureaucratic interests, they said, they often had to fight their own administration. In a similar vein, governors found it difficult at times to gain the support or even the neutrality of professional groups and nonprofit organizations involved in the delivery of services. Groups representing professionals such as teachers, doctors, and social workers often protested changes, while nonprofits welcomed the status quo. Their regulatory status and their ability to secure grant funds made them sensitive to any delivery-system amendments. Special interest groups were able to mask their specific agendas by portraying their positions as in the public interest.

Governors Winter and White, who wanted to make changes in specific strategic areas of concern, had to create their own coalitions either in the legislature, the media, or the general public. Governors, Dreyfus said, often were required to find their own horror stories or anecdotes to counteract the drama and playacting vested interests would stage for the public. Additionally, governors found they often needed to go to the public to win necessary support in the legislature. They had to escalate the dialogue to include statewide interests or values. They had to make the opposition seem to reflect limited self-serving priorities. Sometimes it worked; sometimes it did not. The principal variable determining outcome was often the governor's willingness to go out in front and build alliances among the public, the business community, local officials, and other groups.

Some of the governors proved skillful at splitting off and dividing professional groups and weakening their appeal to the legislature. Divide-and-conquer strategies were not always purposeful. Interest and advocacy groups, while in agreement on some issues, were often not in agreement on all issues. Their differences were sometimes as important as their similarities. Successful governors understood this fact.

Governors found ways to work with professional and advocate groups. Over time, they were able to gain their trust and support. Janklow, for example, willingly dropped teacher testing to gain teacher certification and teacher support. White and Evans won key allies by agreeing to move on salary issues affecting teachers early in their terms. Their efforts, even when not successful, helped win teacher help toward broader educational changes.

Several strategies were used to deal with recalcitrant bureaucracies. Janklow, for example, often forced the issue through a public meeting with his senior appointees. Dreyfus's use of the bull pen and his standing invitation to the press to cover his office made it difficult for agency heads to refuse, at least publicly, to go along with the governor. Snelling seemed to relish frequent meetings with his cabinet and the use of evaluative questions that, to the governor, helped keep the departments on track. But none of the governors found an easy way to get at middle-management civil-service types who were seen, at times, as standing in the way of their policy or program initiatives. They were a protected class and difficult to pressure into position.

Leadership and Permanence

The governors were not sanguine about their ability to guarantee the permanence of their policies or programs. One governor suggested that permanence should not be a real priority. The fact that we live in a democracy and that the electorate deserves the right to vote in changes or midcourse corrections seemed paramount. Other governors wondered whether they or their associates were being responsible if they did not conceive of and initiate strategies to institutionalize their more important changes, such as Winter's educational changes in Mississippi. How could they call what they were doing a reform, one governor asked his colleagues, if what they were doing did not stay in place long enough to achieve results or secure impact?

Institutionalizing programs did not seem as important as institutionalizing the underlying principles governing policies. Most of the governors felt that securing sustained public commitments to the basic values behind their initiatives was essential if specific programs were to survive them. In this context, they viewed their ability to change values or civic culture as crucial. All the studied governors gave William Winter high marks for building a "no-turning-back" attitude into educational change in Mississippi. He was able to convince the power elite, as well as the state's citizenry, that inferior education was bad for the state and bad for each household. He transformed Mississippi's educational ethos.

The governors' capacity to build a public-policy theology around an initiative or change was viewed as essential to a policy's maintenance after the governor's term of office. The Social Security system was viewed as a paradigm. Its leaders, over time, made the values and principles that govern the system difficult, if not politically impossible, to attack. Good leadership, strategic coalition building, publicizing of success stories, tying the initiative to the "best" that is America, and linking the initiative's success to the self-interest of everyone were the activities most seemed to consider essential to creating a new theology. Policy theologies were easier to establish when the state's citizens saw the potential results as significant and as likely to benefit most of them at one time or another.

Leadership and the New Federalism

Most of the studied governors—Republican and Democrat—found the New Federalism wanting. There seemed to be a gap between what the president promised and what he produced. While the governors liked the increased flexibility provided by the block grant approach, most viewed the block grants with a jaundiced eye: "They gave us more freedom and less money."

Most of the governors faulted the New Federalism for not really trying to sort out basic responsibilities among all levels of government in a fair and efficient manner. New Federalism, they said, proved really to be a code term for budget cutting, rather than a true shifting and sorting out of responsibilities and regulatory authority.

Significant amendments to the federal system are still required "if states are to fulfill a major social welfare role in a proactive policy way," said one governor, "We still have not defined appropriate federal and state roles regarding health, education and welfare. Hell, we don't even have good criteria to establish roles and responsibilities."

Many of the initiatives of the governors and their states in the health, education, and welfare areas should foster a reevaluation of the textbook assertion that policy change in this nation occurs primarily in increments. Some initiatives were important and seemed to provide a major break from the past. Mississippi and Texas's efforts to restructure education, for example, as well as Massachusetts's health and welfare initiatives, reflect major departures from existing state and, federal public policies. They also lend themselves to replication nationally and in other states. States may have once again become what Justice Brandeis asserted they should be: laboratories for the nation.

Index